SA8000

SA8000

the definitive guide to the new social standard

Deborah Leipziger

FINANCIAL TIMES
Prentice Hall

An imprint of **Pearson Education**

London / New York / San Francisco / Toronto / Sydney / Tokyo / Singapore
Hong Kong / Cape Town / Madrid / Paris / Milan / Munich / Amsterdam

PEARSON EDUCATION LIMITED

Head Office:
Edinburgh Gate
Harlow CM20 2JE
Tel: +44 (0)1279 623623
Fax: +44 (0)1279 431059

London Office:
128 Long Acre, London WC2E 9AN
Tel: +44 (0)20 7447 2000
Fax: +44 (0)20 7240 5771
Website: www.business-minds.com

First published in Great Britain in 2001

The right of Deborah Leipziger to be identified as author of this work has been
asserted by her in accordance with the Copyright, Designs and Patents Act 1988.

ISBN 0 273 65377 6

British Library Cataloguing in Publication Data
A CIP catalogue record for this book can be obtained from the British Library.

10 9 8 7 6 5 4 3 2 1

Typeset by Northern Phototypesetting Co. Ltd, Bolton
Printed and bound in Great Britain by Biddles Ltd, Guildford & King's Lynn

The Publishers' policy is to use paper manufactured from sustainable forests.

About the author

As European Director for Social Accountability International, Deborah Leipziger played a central role in developing the standard Social Accountability 8000 and its Guidance Document.

Deborah Leipziger is also the co-author of *Corporate Citizenship: Successful Strategies of Responsible Companies*. A native of Brazil, Deborah has a Masters in Public Administration from Columbia University. She resides in The Hague (Netherlands), where she is the proud mother of Natasha Lara, Alexandra Nicole and Jacqueline Lucia.

This book is dedicated to Daryl A. Mundis, my husband and friend, and to my daughter Natasha Lara who inspires me with her *joie de vivre,* and to Jacqueline Lucia and Alexandra Nicole, who were born in the midst of Chapter 5.

Readers should note that SA8000, referred to throughout this book, is a registered trademark of Social Accountability International.

Contents

Acknowledgements

Like SA8000, this book has benefited from the perspective of many people in several continents and from a wide range of sectors. It is impossible to acknowledge the people who made this book a reality without first recognizing the people behind SA8000. SA8000 owes its genesis to the hard work and determination of Alice Tepper Marlin President of Social Accountability International (SAI). Alice has played a key role in the development of the field of corporate social responsibility. Under her leadership and guidance, the field of corporate social responsibility has gone from a hippie fad to an issue that occupies the minds of even the most conservative of boardrooms. She has been an important influence and mentor in my professional development, a fact for which I am especially appreciative. I am also particularly grateful for the countless hours she has spent editing this book and important insights that she provided.

In 1994, the International Labour Organization's International Programme for the Elimination of Child Labour (IPEC) gave me a grant to assess what companies were doing to address child labor and what strategies they might adopt. From this initial project, carried out while I was the Director of International Programs at the Council on Economic Priorities (the sister organization of SAI), came the idea of a universal standard with a system of independent verification. With funding from the ILO grant, the Council on Economic Priorities brought together companies for a roundtable discussion. The corporate leaders who advised the Council to host such discussions deserve recognition for their foresight. Among this group of pioneers, several deserve a special mention: Fitz Hilaire of Avon, Johannes Merck of Otto Versand, David Zwiebel of Eileen Fisher, Doriane Beyer of the US Child Labor Federation and Tom DeLuca of Toys "R" Us. Neil Kearney, of the International Textile, Garment and Leather Workers' Federation and his relentless crusade on behalf of workers around the world has been an inspiration. The entire Advisory Board of SAI (listed in the Appendix) deserves a standing ovation for their tireless work to develop and promote the standard.

Several individuals at SAI deserve recognition for their contributions to developing the SA8000 standard and for their generous assistance with this book. Eileen Kohl Kaufman, the Executive Director of SAI, has worked ceaselessly to promote SA8000 around the world and I am grateful for her insights, encouragement and friendship. I am especially grateful to Shareen Hertel for her friendship and dedication to this cause and her ability as wordsmith, which played a major role in developing the standard. Judy Gearhart of SAI deserves special mention for playing a major role in the development of the Guidance Document and the regional consultations. Sharon Powell has been a terrific help in keeping me informed and connected to SAI. I am also very grateful to Sir Geoffrey Chandler for his assistance in promoting SA8000 and to Teresa Fabian, formerly of CEP London, for her friendship and hard work to get SA8000 and the Private Sector Working Group up and running.

Many people reviewed this book and provided brilliant comments, among them are:

Dorianne Beyer
Doug DeRouisseau
Dominique Gangneux
Judy Gearhart
Jeff Horner
Eileen Kohl Kaufman
Neil Kearney
Eammon Malloy
Alice Tepper Marlin
Tina Stick
Hillary Sutcliffe
Raj Thamotheram
Piet den Toom
David Zwiebel.

The following people reviewed the case study of their own company:

Tom DeLuca
Bertrand Duliscouet

Amy Hall
Sharon Hayes
Fitz Hilaire
Jouko Kuisma
Achim Lohrie
Frits Nagel
Marisa Parmigiani.

I am most grateful to David Zwiebel and Rochelle Zaid for developing the majority of the forms in Chapter 4.

A special thanks also to Joe Spieler, my agent, for his assistance and persistence in bringing this book to life and to Bert Koot for his assistance with my computers, printers and for the installation of software in both Dutch and English.

Pradeep Jethi, of FT Management, first saw the need for such a book and I am grateful to him for all of his assistance and support both on this book and on *Corporate Citizenship*. Richard Stagg, Helena Dahlstrom, Linda Dhondy and Michela Rossi of Pearson Education continue to provide valuable input.

And to my friends who have sustained me through the most incredible year and throughout this project: Monica Sallouti, Hazel Kidd, Jane Stephenson, Christina Burgers Wilson, Susan Martin, Deb Vernet, Robin Schaap, Ann Marie Armbruster, Karin Green, and Sasa Vaugham. Your encouragement has been a gift and I thank you.

To my parents, Fabia and Michael, and my brother, David, who have taught me by example the importance of making the world a better place.

Above all, I owe a special debt of gratitude to my husband, Daryl Mundis, who has always supported my vision and who has worked tirelessly with me on this book and in his own field to make the world a more humane place.

Foreword

Few books have the potential to change the way in which companies operate. *SA8000: The Definitive Guide to the New Social Standard* is one such book: with the power not only to change companies, but to improve the lives of workers around the world.

Toys "R" Us believes in SA8000 because we believe in children. We at Toys "R" Us understand that each child matters. Each child makes a difference. We are a company built around children and their needs. For us, children make the world go around. This commitment to children led us to SA8000, as a way to ensure that our toys and products are made in ways which promote the well-being of families. The rise in child labor and other abuses of human rights led Toys "R" Us to draw a line in the sand. We are committed to working with our 3,000 suppliers and their sub-suppliers to ensure that they share our values and concern for the well-being of children.

We are working with SA8000 because it is the right thing to do.

We also believe that SA8000 makes business sense. As our suppliers come into conformance with SA8000, we expect that we will continue to notice business benefits, as well as social benefits. SA8000 allows us to improve our ability to manage our supply chain and to ensure optimal product quality.

Toys "R" Us has played a significant role in the development of the standard, Social Accountability 8000, for several years. Why does Toys "R" Us work to promote SA8000? For several reasons. First, consumers are becoming more concerned about social issues. A recent study by Environics of Canada, in association with the Prince of Wales Business Leaders' Forum and the Conference Board of the US surveyed 25,000 people in 23 countries and found that consumers around the world are concerned about the social responsibility of corporations. Two-thirds of the people polled in the USA, UK, Japan and Germany consider ethical behavior as more important than making profits or creating jobs. Some 79 percent of the people polled felt that large companies should be held "completely responsible" for protecting the health and safety of workers and 72 percent for avoiding child labor. We believe that our consumers are very concerned about social issues. Studies show that young consumers are especially committed to social issues.

Toys "R" Us believes that SA8000 is good for the bottom line, as it will allow us to find suppliers that share our values. A supplier that does not care about the health and safety of its workers is more likely to produce poor quality products. Because it focuses on management systems, we think SA8000 can be a tool for suppliers, allowing them to increase productivity and worker morale.

I predict that in the next decade, corporate social responsibility will continue to grow in importance. SA8000 will become the standard by which all companies are judged. *SA8000: The Definitive Guide to the New Social Standard* will help your company to implement strong social standards.

Tom DeLuca, VP for Product Development and Safety Assurance
Toys "R" Us

Preface

Social Accountability 8000 is a global standard designed to make workplaces socially responsible. Based on conventions of the International Labour Organization, SA8000 is already being adopted in 12 countries. The Standard addresses issues such as discrimination, health and safety, child labor, and compensation. Some of the world's leading companies are adopting the SA8000 model, including Toys "R" Us, Avon, Otto Versand, and Dole Food Company Inc. Together the SA8000 companies represent annual revenues of $106 billion.

What makes SA8000 a breakthrough? SA8000:

- is the first auditable standard on workers' rights;
- is already operational;
- creates management systems for implementation;
- provides concise definitions of key terms;
- is global;
- can be applied to many sectors;
- is based on the ISO model, making it easier to integrate with quality and/or environmental audits;
- was developed by business, non-governmental organizations, and trade unions.

Companies around the world are finding that SA8000 is not only good for the community, but it is good for business as well. SA8000 can help your company to minimize risk while promoting:

- productivity and quality
- employee retention

- management systems
- improved supply chain management, and
- new markets and new customers.

This book acts as a road map for companies seeking to implement SA8000. Through case studies, companies are introduced to some of the lessons learned from companies working to the SA8000 standard. The book addresses some of the most complex social questions facing companies: how to determine what constitutes a living wage and how to address social issues in China. SA8000 is discussed provision by provision, introducing basic elements and issues and drawing on the policies, strategies, job descriptions, and plans of major global companies.

There is a common misperception that only the South, or developing countries, can benefit from the implementation of SA8000. The reality is that the industrialized North also stands to gain from the adoption of SA8000. There are significant abuses of workers' rights in the industrialized countries, as well as in the developing world. Immigrants in world capitals such as New York City and London, who don't speak the country's language or know their legal rights, are subject to exploitation, just as they might be in their home countries, often with very little recourse.

In implementing SA8000, it is important to understand the regional issues that may affect implementation. Regional difficulties, however, cannot be used as an excuse for overlooking elements of the standard. SA8000 must be applied as a whole, regardless of location. Each region presents its own challenges to implementation. This book provides insights on social issues in six major regions: Asia, Latin America, Africa, Eastern Europe, Western Europe and North America.

What is the future of social accountability? There are efforts underway to link social auditing with environmental and quality auditing. Considered the "holy grail" of auditing, integrated and combined audits are currently being developed. Such audits will present challenges and opportunities for training and the development of management systems.

SA8000 was developed to provide a single, global standard on workers' rights. Over the course of several years, a number of standards have emerged that are either national or regional and/or sectoral. The multiplicity of standards is confusing to suppliers who have to work in a morass of acronyms. Few companies operate in one sector alone or in one market. As workplaces around the world are audited, companies will seek to alert consumers to the progress being made in the social arena. There is a danger that the wide range of codes will confuse consumers, which could lead to indifference and skepticism. Convergence is imperative for both consumers and suppliers alike.

Introduction

Social Accountability 8000 is a code of conduct for companies seeking to make the workplace more humane. Unlike other codes, SA8000 is a global code that can be implemented in any country and in any sector.

This book is a road map for companies seeking to adopt SA8000. Dozens of companies have shared their practical experience in improving workplace standards. Avon Products, Otto Versand, Co-op Italia, and Dole Food Products Inc. are among the companies profiled in case studies. These companies share the lessons they have learned in implementing SA8000 and describe the challenges they have faced.

This book includes the following tools:

- sample policies
- sample forms
- sample job descriptions
- checklists to test if the company is audit-ready
- best practices.

This book is written for the manager tasked with implementing SA8000 or other social codes at a facility. It can also be used by companies, government agencies and non-profit organizations seeking to bring their suppliers into compliance with the SA8000 standard. The book is also helpful for executives considering whether or not to adopt SA8000. Consultants advising companies can also benefit from the case studies and practices described in this book. Likewise, interested parties, such as non-government organizations (NGOs) and trade unions, can benefit from this book by gaining perspective on the complexity of implementing management systems. Interested parties seeking to influence companies and to encourage them to implement SA8000 will also find this book helpful.

The field of social accountability is evolving rapidly. New definitions are emerging and best practice is being continuously redefined. For example, a few years ago, companies with codes of conduct were considered leaders. Now, ten years later, a code is not enough, there is a need for third party audits. The dynamic nature of the field makes such a book a necessity. It also requires that an electronic version of the book be developed to accommodate changes. The ability to download material and to share it with suppliers will be most valuable. We hope that the website can be interactive, and that users can share their lessons learned.

Because this is a new field, there is a lack of qualified consultants to advise companies on implementing SA8000. Moreover, auditors are not allowed to provide consulting services to the firms that they audit, due to conflicts of interest. While some consultants do exist, their main qualification may be the SA8000 training course.

How to use this book

This book is a how-to guide, a manual for implementation. As such, it can be read cover-to-cover, or the reader can read the sections that are most relevant. Like SA8000 itself, there is a high degree of inter-relatedness between each section. Where relevant information is located in another chapter, the reader is encouraged to follow the author's note to view the relevant section in another chapter.

This book is written in a concise and user-friendly manner to allow busy managers to easily access material. The discussions on human rights, regional concerns, and interested parties merit greater detail. Rather than repeat material that is already available on these topics, resources are listed in the Appendix.

There are many tools available to companies seeking to adopt SA8000: the *SA8000 Guidance Document*, training programs, and the Social Accountability International website. This book should be used in conjunction with the *SA8000 Guidance Document*, which interprets the standard. Keep in mind that the *Guidance Document*, primarily written for the auditor, has a different focus from this book, which is intended for a manager tasked with implementation.

Social Accountability International (SAI) offers training and accredits training programs all over the world. Like the *Guidance Document*, the training programs are also geared both to auditors and managers. For information on training, check the SAI website: www.sa-intl.org.

Contents overview

The book offers the following information.

Chapter 1 provides a basic definition of SA8000 and what makes it a breakthrough. The chapter also outlines the business benefits of SA8000 and the cost of non-compliance. The International Organization for Standardization (ISO) systems and their contrasts and similarities to SA8000 are also explained in this section. This chapter contains a series of frequently-asked questions (and answers) about SA8000, including a segment on other initiatives to improve working conditions around the world and how they compare to SA8000.

Chapter 2 contains case studies of SA8000 companies, including what lessons the companies learned about social accountability and what challenges they faced. Each case study focuses on why the company decided to implement SA8000, how it works with its suppliers to ensure implementation, and what benefits it has noticed as a result of adopting SA8000. These case studies are a result of questionnaires sent to the companies and interviews with key personnel. One of the key themes to emerge is the different types of experiences and challenges each company describes, based on the sector(s) and region(s) in which they operate.

Chapter 3 provides background on the International Labour Organization and its conventions, which serve as the starting point for SA8000. It also provides background on the key sections of SA8000: child labor, forced labor, health and safety, freedom of association and the right to collective bargaining, discrimination, disciplinary practices, working hours, and compensation. The links between each section of the standard are also provided.

Chapter 4 provides a manual for implementing the management systems of SA8000. This chapter provides information on how to develop a social accountability policy, the responsibilities of SA8000 representatives, controlling suppliers, conducting risk analysis, addressing concerns and taking corrective actions, training, and maintaining records. The chapter includes sample policies.

Chapter 5 describes the importance of working with interested parties (IPs), such as NGOs and trade unions. In addition to providing case studies of some IPs, the chapter illustrates the challenges and rewards of working with IPs.

Chapter 6 contains an overview of the regional issues surrounding SA8000 in Asia, Latin America, Africa, Eastern Europe, Western Europe, and North America. This chapter describes the unique challenges of each region, and highlights some of the issues for specific countries within each region.

Chapter 7 describes why and how companies communicate with stakeholders and the public about SA8000. What type of information needs to be disclosed? To whom? In what form? To what end? The chapter concludes with examples of guides to best practices in social reporting: AccountAbility 1000 and the Global Reporting Initiative.

Chapter 8 asks: what does an SA8000 world look like? This chapter examines the potential for integrated audits, which link social, environmental, and/or quality. The chapter also examines the potential for the convergence of social standards and challenges for the SA8000 system. The book concludes with a focus on partnerships, the rise of a hybrid auditor and the potential impact of new legislation.

How this book developed

There is a great demand for expertise on how to implement SA8000. Suppliers are tasked with developing systems and understanding complex issues. This book benefited tremendously from an internal supplier handbook developed by David Zwiebel and Rochelle Zaid at Eileen Fisher, which was used as a starting point.

Questionnaires were sent to companies in Europe, North America, and Latin America and to their suppliers in Asia. Twenty companies responded to questionnaires about their implementation of SA8000. Extensive interviews were conducted with company managers, decision-makers, academics, NGOs, auditors, and trade union representatives. Each company case study was reviewed by relevant staff to ensure accuracy.

The author welcomes feedback on the book and lessons learned at her email address: thehague@wanadoo.nl or at SAI (info@sa-intl.org).

Chapter 1 describes SA8000 and provides a rationale for why companies should adopt the standard. The benefits of compliance are detailed, as is the cost of non-compliance. Note that it is difficult to get good data on the benefits of compliance, since it is difficult to isolate the benefits of the system from other factors, such as new management and economic factors. This chapter also includes a section which contrasts SA8000 with ISO systems. The final section of this chapter contrasts the different codes of conduct that are emerging.

1

What is SA8000?

Social Accountability 8000 is a global, verifiable standard for managing auditing and certifying compliance with workplace issues. Based on conventions of the International Labour Organization and related international human rights instruments – including the Universal Declaration of Human Rights and the UN Declaration on the Rights of the Child – SA8000 seeks to assure the basic rights of workers.

SA8000 is a voluntary code of conduct. Companies are choosing to implement SA8000 as a means of enhancing their reputations by improving workplace conditions and because they want to do the right thing. Pressure from consumers and investors also plays a key role in encouraging companies to adopt SA8000.

To certify compliance with SA8000, qualified auditors visit facilities regularly to assess performance on a wide range of specific issues: child labor, health and safety, freedom of association, the right to collective bargaining, disciplinary practices, working hours, and compensation. Auditors also evaluate management systems to verify ongoing compliance. If the auditor detects "nonconformities" management has to identify the root cause, correct the non-conformity and put in place preventative action to prevent recurrence. Facilities need to abide by a timetable for addressing problems; they must document performance in all areas and accredited auditors must verify compliance.

What makes SA8000 a breakthrough? The SA8000 standard:

- is the first auditable standard on workers' rights;
- is already operational;
- creates management systems for implementation;
- provides concise definitions of key terms;
- is global;
- can be applied to many sectors;
- is based on the ISO model, making it easier to integrate with ISO quality and/or environmental audits;
- was developed by business, NGOs, and trade unions.

The business benefits

SA8000 strengthens communities by improving conditions in the workplace but can SA8000 provide benefits to your company? Research and anecdotal evidence show that there are significant business benefits to companies implementing the standard. Among these benefits are:

- greater employee retention and enhanced performance;
- enhanced product quality and productivity;
- improved management;
- enhanced supply chain management;
- protection of reputation;
- development of new markets and new customers.

Greater employee retention and enhanced performance

"SA8000 has given us a formal method to publicly communicate to our employees, our customers, and to our suppliers the principles by which we manage our company. Our employees have expressed a positive response to this program."

Peter Venenma, Chairman and CEO, L.E. Jones[1]

By treating workers with dignity and allowing them to have a greater voice in the workplace, SA8000 boosts the morale of employees – which can have a significant impact on productivity and quality. Higher employee morale leads to greater rates of retention, which cuts the costs of recruiting and training new staff.

A number of companies implementing SA8000 are reporting better employee morale as a result of SA8000. WE Europe, a Dutch clothing company, is among the companies noticing this effect. Celtipharm, a French pharmaceutical company, has found SA8000 to be a useful part of the hiring process. The company is expanding rapidly and uses SA8000 to ascertain the values of prospective employees and to see if there is an alignment of values. When asked about their values, two-thirds of those interviewed had no reply. Those candidates who had a response were introduced to SA8000 during the interview process to ascertain which candidates would support their company's goals and values.[2]

"By continually conversing with the employees about the firm and raising its profile in the community, M. Guerin (President of Celtipharm) feels that they have been able to develop pride and loyalty within the company and credibility in the eyes of outsiders, using SA8000 as a management tool to achieve these ends."[3]

Enhanced product quality and productivity

The introduction of better management systems can boost product quality and overall productivity. Likewise, improvements in the health and safety arena can have an effect on product as well. For example, eliminating chemicals that are toxic to workers can ensure that the final product is safer.

Reducing defects and accidents enhances product quality. SA8000, with its focus on management systems, leads to a more efficient workplace. Moreover, by eliminating structural over-time and providing for one day off in seven, the introduction of SA8000 leads to a workforce that is less fatigued, and therefore less likely to cause accidents or defects on the production line. As children are substituted with adults, quality rises.

SA8000, WITH ITS FOCUS ON MANAGEMENT SYSTEMS, LEADS TO A MORE EFFICIENT WORKPLACE

WE Europe reports higher productivity as a result of SA8000. This could be a result of better management systems or higher employee morale. New Balance Athletic Shoe, Inc. has reported an increase of nearly 25 percent in productivity after it cut work-hours among its suppliers in China. Some Chinese workers work 80 hours per week during busy seasons.[4]

Enhanced management

Once established, the management systems of SA8000 will strengthen the business. Providing training, defining responsibility and developing manuals will strengthen the management of the company. While these will take a considerable amount of time to implement, the benefits over the long term are considerable.

Through its management systems, SA8000 formalizes policies that may already be in existence, but not systematized. L.E. Jones, a small US manufacturing company, noted that in the process of implementing SA8000, they updated and developed controls for policies and procedures already in place.

"SA8000 registration efforts had the unexpected benefit of highlighting this weakness."[5]

Quality of management is often cited by financial markets and the media as what differentiates a good company from a great company. One can speculate that a company can demonstrate the quality of its management by its understanding of its supply chain and by the introduction of effective management systems. It is possible to extrapolate that companies that show leadership in social areas, have leadership potential in other areas. The opposite of this also holds – that companies with poor social records cut corners in other areas as well, compromising not only on employee safety but also on equipment.

Enhanced supply chain management

The supply chains of major retailers and multinational corporations are long, complex, and multi-layered. Before they began to implement SA8000, some companies were unaware of the full extent of their supply chain. The process of communicating with suppliers leads to greater clarity and better supply chain management. The standard also serves to weed out suppliers with poor performance who may be engaging in illegal practices.

There is growing evidence that improving supply-chain management can be beneficial to the company. Mark Goyder of Tomorrow's Company is studying supply chain management and states that there is "growing evidence for the close linkage between values and value."[6] His research shows that this is a time of significant change for suppliers. Companies are forming relationships with strategic suppliers and decreasing their supplier base. Suppliers are operating in a more competitive market, with changing technology and increased pressure to deliver "Just in Time."[7]

According to Goyder, better supply chain management can have the following business benefits:

- "reduced transaction costs
- increased profitability, in some cases shared profitability
- material cost reduction
- reduced costs as a result of a reduced need to switch suppliers, and
- increased competitiveness in the marketplace from improved relationships."[8]

Tomorrow's Company has conducted workshops with companies in the UK and the findings demonstrate an important convergence with SA8000 and better supply chain management. These findings suggest that:

"All the company's relationships impact upon each other. Devising best supplier relationship strategies in isolation of concurrent work on employee and customer relationships will deliver gains that are partial at best."[9] SA8000 is such an integrated system, linking suppliers, employees, and customers into a common framework and a common language.

According to Frits Nagel of WE Europe, the relationship between a retailer and its suppliers is built on trust. SA8000 allows companies to define and align its values with those of its suppliers. According to Marie-Pierre Daniel, Celtipharm's General Secretary,

"A large part of the appeal of SA8000 was the way that it formalized their ethical stance."[10]

The company uses SA8000 as a starting point to discuss the company's values with suppliers.

Protection of reputation

"All multinational corporations should recognize that the world is now watching. The bigger and more recognizable the company, the more likely it will face exposure for infraction of human rights. Furthermore, the largest companies have the most to lose. There are the obvious risks of lawsuits and fines, but even more significant is the potential loss of reputation – a significant portion of most companies' value. Of particular interest to corporate executives and boards of directors is their personal exposure to shareholder derivative lawsuits for not

having policies in place to protect the corporation from such scandals and the subsequent loss of reputational value."[11]

> Brad Brown, Susan Perry, John Wheeler, University of Virginia

Adherence to SA8000 prevents problems and violations from occurring. Fines, exposés, and lost business that could result from negative exposure can be prevented with careful implementation of SA8000. While some other codes also promise this, SA8000 is better at preventing risk because it has an inbuilt system of checks and balances through the accreditation process and through the appeals system. By preventing risk, some SA8000 members are finding it easier to attract venture capital.

SA8000 can also help companies stay ahead of regulations. What is voluntary today may well become a matter of legislation in the coming years.

Create new markets, attract new customers

De Nadai, a Brazilian catering company, credits SA8000 with attracting new clients. Why is this the case? SA8000 provides companies with the ability to differentiate themselves in a crowded marketplace. With the advent of globalization, companies have more competitors – being socially accountable, and being able to prove that you are – is a mechanism for differentiating your business.

SA8000 can also help to keep customers loyal to your company. Avon sees SA8000 as a valuable marketing tool, which provides the transparency consumers want.[12]

SA8000 as a career enhancement tool

Just as SA8000 gives companies a higher profile in a global economy, it can also make employees more visible within a large company. Because of his commitment to SA8000, Fitz Hilaire of Avon reports that he is now seen as an "intrapreneur." By spearheading Avon's implementation of the standard, Fitz has had more opportunities to work directly with the most senior people within the company.

The costs of SA8000

There are several types of costs associated with SA8000:

- the cost of the audit[13]
- the cost of preparing for an audit
- the cost of taking corrective measures, and
- the cost of non-compliance, i.e. the cost of doing nothing.

The cost of non-compliance

We live in a world with no hiding places. The news media has indelibly placed in the minds of consumers the image of children working, of exploitative working conditions, of protesters. Activists have focused on Nike, accusing the company's suppliers of abusing workers' rights in Asia. Kathie Lee Gifford, one of America's most popular talk show hosts, cried on national television when confronted with evidence that a child had made a product that bears her name.

One thing is certain – consumers view companies as responsible for how their products are made, regardless of where. **In a recent study of 25,000 people in 23 countries, 79 percent felt that large companies should be held "completely responsible" for protecting the health and safety of workers.**[14]

What are the costs of non-compliance?

A weakened brand

In a global economy, brands are increasingly important. A brand name seeks to build loyalty and confidence, which allegations of abuses can destroy. Activists often seek out the most well-known brands in launching a campaign.

Sales

When a brand comes under fire, sales can suffer. According to Price-waterhouseCoopers, four out of ten global consumers boycotted a company they considered to be unethical.[15]

Legal bills

Taking companies to court is becoming more popular. **There is a growing trend of multinational companies being sued in the country of their headquarters for abuses in developing countries.** Rio Tinto was sued in the UK for an alleged case of uranium poisoning in Namibia by its subsidiary Rossing Uranium. According to the judge in the case:

"This is a case in which, having regard to the nature of the litigation, substantial justice cannot be done in the appropriate forum (Namibia), but can be done where the resources are available."[16]

In July 2000, the House of Lords allowed South African workers to sue Cape in the UK courts for health problems due to asbestos, contracted in South Africa. The *Financial Times* reported that

"any multinational with its parent company in England will be liable to be sued here, (in the UK) in respect of its activities anywhere in the world."[17]

Adopting SA8000 has the potential to decrease a company's legal bills. At a time when law suits against companies are rising, these savings can be dramatic, albeit hard to quantify. In the UK, the Trades Union Congress reports that awards for sex and race discrimination or illegal termination are increasing, while awards are doubling in value.[18]

Share price

A weakened brand, falling sales, and sky-rocketing legal bills can impact share price dramatically.

As in the case of assessing the benefits of compliance, the cost of non-compliance is difficult to calculate. It is hard to measure what might have happened if the company had taken a different course of action or what factors are responsible for a fall in sales or in share price.

How can SA8000 be used?

SA8000 is a versatile tool which can be used in several different ways through either first party, second party, or third party assessments.

First party assessment

This describes what happens when a company conducts an internal assessment of its activities. This type of self-assessment is often done in anticipation of an audit by a certification company. However, a first party assessment alone does not indicate that the company is certified. The common term for first party assessment is *monitoring*.

Second party assessment

This term applies when a company audits its suppliers. For example, a toy manufacturer might conduct second party assessments of its suppliers' compliance with the SA8000 standard or hire an auditor to do so. A second party assessment does not constitute certification to SA8000, but should be helpful in preparing for one.

Third party assessment

This type of assessment takes place when a company is audited by an independent and external body. The certifying body must be accredited by Social Accountability International, SAI. If the company demonstrates that it complies with SA8000, then the certification firm grants it a certificate. Commonly, facilities implement corrective actions in the process of earning a certificate.

SA8000 compared with ISO standards

In addition to drawing from conventions of the International Labour Organization, the SA8000 system is modelled after the ISO9000 and ISO14000 series of standards for quality control and environmental management systems. These ISO standards are successfully used at several hundred thousand facilities around the world. SA8000 resembles the ISO series in that both require management systems that aim at continuous improvement. Both systems are based on a similar methodology for auditors and for accreditation bodies. However, there are several differences between SA8000 and the ISO series, as Fig. 1.1 indicates. First, unlike ISO standards, SA8000 has performance provisions; management systems alone are not enough to ensure conformance with SA8000. Second, ISO standards are initially developed at the national level and then harmonized by the International

Standards Organization in Geneva, while SA8000 was developed as a global standard from the beginning. Third, interviews with workers play a more significant role in an SA8000 audit than in ISO audits, because of the focus of the standard on workers' rights. Fourth, the components of SA8000 are highly inter-related. For example, low wages may be linked to higher incidences of child labor. The implications of these inter-relationships are explored in greater depth in Chapter 3.[19]

Figure 1.1 ■ Differences between ISO standards and SA8000

ISO	SA8000
Management systems criteria	Performance criteria and management systems
Standards developed first at national level and then harmonized	Global standard from the beginning
Less focus on interviews with workers	Interviews with workers constitute evidence, key focus of audit
Generally, each section of standard is distinct	Sections of standard are inter-related

SA8000 performance criteria

As previously mentioned, SA8000 has performance criteria. Companies must follow national law or international norms, whichever is higher. Other performance criteria include the following.

Child labor

SA8000 prohibits child labor, under the age of 15 in most cases. Certified companies must assure the education of children who might lose their jobs as a result of the standard.

Forced labor

SA8000 prohibits forced labor. Workers cannot be required to surrender their identity papers or pay "deposits" as a condition of employment.

Health and safety

Companies must meet basic standards for a safe and healthy working environment, including safe drinking water, clean rest-room facilities, applicable safety equipment, and necessary training.

Freedom of association

SA8000 respects the rights of workers to form and join trade unions and to bargain collectively, without fear of reprisals.

Discrimination

SA8000 bans discrimination on the basis of race, caste, national origin, religion, disability, gender, sexual orientation, union membership, or political affiliation.

Disciplinary practices

SA8000 forbids corporal punishment, mental or physical coercion and verbal abuse of workers.

Working hours

SA8000 provides for a maximum 48-hour working week, with at least one day off per week, and a cap of 12 hours of over-time per week,[20] remunerated at a premium rate.

Compensation

Wages paid must meet all minimum legal standards and provide sufficient income for basic needs, with at least some discretionary income.

Management

SA8000 defines procedures and effective management implementation and review of SA8000 compliance, from designating responsible personnel to keeping records, addressing concerns, and taking corrective action.

In addition to meeting the above criteria, facilities must comply with relevant national and local legislation.

How SA8000 developed

In the early to mid 1990s, many companies were developing their own codes of conduct, but often without monitoring or external verification. Even in cases where there was monitoring of supplier factories, it was difficult to ensure consistency across audits. Suppliers were increasingly confused by the myriad codes of conduct, many of which had different requirements. In some cases, the same suppliers were being audited by different companies. Consumers and civil society were suspicious about companies auditing themselves and demanded greater transparency. There was a high degree of inconsistency among codes.

In 1994, the International Labour Organization's International Programme on the Elimination of Child Labour (IPEC) commissioned a staff member of the Council on Economic Priorities (CEP) to study what measures companies were taking to address the problem of child labor. CEP convened a meeting of major companies to discuss how companies were seeking to combat child labor and what measures they might take to address this serious abuse of human rights. The companies present at the CEP consultation expressed an interest in discussing possible joint approaches to improving workers' rights. At the behest of these companies, CEP convened regular consultations in both New York and London between 1995 and 1997.

In 1996, CEP established an international Advisory Board of NGOs, trade unions, and the private sector to develop a global standard. Approximately half of the Advisory Board is from the corporate sector, while the other half represents civil society, including trade unions and experts on workers' rights and human rights. In early 1997, CEP established an accreditation agency, now known as Social Accountability International (SAI). SAI's mission is to enable organizations to be socially accountable by:

- convening key stakeholders to develop voluntary social accountability standards;
- accrediting qualified bodies to verify compliance with SAI standards;
- promoting awareness and understanding of SAI standards, while promoting implementation at a global level.

SAI audits the auditors, but does not grant certifications to the SA8000 standard.

An SA8000 Advisory Board composed of representatives from NGOs, companies, academia, and unions meets regularly to review and revise the standard and advise on accreditation applications. SAI is funded by charitable contributions from philanthropies and government and also earns revenues from royalties, sales of publications, training, conferences, memberships, and the accreditation of auditors, course providers, and certification firms.

SAI is an affiliate of the Council on Economic Priorities (CEP), a pioneer in the field of corporate social responsibility. Founded in 1969, CEP's mission is to provide accurate and impartial analysis to evaluate corporate social performance and to promote excellence in corporate citizenship. For more than three decades, CEP has rated corporate performance to provide consumers and investors with information and tools for change.

A word on terminology

SAI *accredits* certification bodies.

Certification companies (such as SGS, BVQI, UL, ITs and DNV) *certify* compliance with SA8000, facility by facility. Non-governmental organizations (NGOs) also qualify. Companies that commit to requiring certification of their suppliers and their own production facilities can become SA8000 signatory members.

Commonly asked questions about SA8000

Why doesn't SA8000 address environmental issues?

Over the course of several decades, environmental standards have become well defined, whereas social standards are still in the process of being fully articulated. SA8000 seeks to provide definitions, standards, and management systems for addressing workers' rights because these issues have not been addressed in an auditable standard. The people who drafted SA8000 sought to innovate, rather than reinvent or duplicate existing work. There are many social issues that are not addressed by SA8000, such as animal welfare and charitable contributions. SAI considers all these issues to be of great importance, but wanted to develop a standard that was focused enough to be realisitic. Several of the companies working with SA8000 are implementing SA8000 together with environmental codes and/or standards to promote ethical behavior. SAI may develop other standards, designing them to be fully compatible with SA8000.

Why is there such an interest in workers' rights? Hasn't this been a problem for centuries? Why is it that companies are taking action now?

Globalization and the rise in telecommunications have changed the business world and created a need for workplace standards. Globalization allows companies to produce goods anywhere in the world. The emergence of a global assembly line has led countries to lower standards in order to attract new production. This race to the bottom has caused workplace standards to fall. New telecommunications technologies have made it commonplace for abuses of workers' rights to be broadcast around the world, as companies can no longer hide poor practices.

Globalization and enhanced communication has led to an important trend: the rise in the influence of non-governmental organizations (NGOs), such as Amnesty International, Oxfam, and Greenpeace. These groups can mobilize media, consumers, and other groups around the world. Effective campaigns by such groups can expose a company with bad practice, causing harm to their reputation and to their bottom line.

Globalization and the advent of the Internet have also created new conditions for businesses: there are more competitors. Hence reputation is becoming more important than ever before. A number of companies view adherence to SA8000 as a mechanism for protecting their brand and for differentiating them in a crowded marketplace.

How much does an SA8000 audit cost and who pays for the cost of the audit?

The cost of the audit depends on several factors including the number of employees at the facility being audited, the country in which it is located, and the travel time for the auditor(s). The cost of the audit is usually borne by the company being certified as the benefits accrue to it. Some companies are paying for the audits of their suppliers, including Toys "R"

Us, Eileen Fisher, and Cutter & Buck. Many companies view the costs associated with SA8000 as an investment in the future.

What is the relationship between SA8000 and the International Labour Organization (ILO)?

The ILO is an agency of the United Nations, and has a tri-partite structure, with representation from unions, national associations of companies, and governments. The ILO has played a significant role in promoting workers' rights through the development of many conventions. These conventions are ratified by countries, not companies. The ILO's mandate is to work at the national level, not the company level. SA8000 works at the company level.

SA8000 is based on many key ILO conventions. While the ILO does not endorse specific codes of conduct, it looks favorably on initiatives which promote the rights of workers. According to Armand Pereira of the ILO Office in Brazil, SA8000 is among the better initiatives, as it refers to the seven core ILO conventions, while involving a wide range of stakeholders in its development.[21]

Since there is no label on a product made in a certified facility, how are consumers informed?

Companies can display their SA8000 certificate in much the same way that they might display an ISO certificate – in their office, on documents such as their annual reports, letterhead, trucks, etc. Companies also plan to advertise their SA8000 certificates through reports and other publications.[22] The SA8000 logo can be on a hang tag or packaging, as long as it is clear that it's the facility where the product was made, and not the item itself, that has been certified.

How can SA8000 be implemented in China, where there are no independent NGOs, or in countries where there are no independent unions or where such activity is illegal?

It is in the very countries where freedoms are most restricted that SA8000 is most needed. Hence SA8000 includes elements which focus on promoting workplace freedoms in areas where they are non-existent or limited. For example, in places where trade unions do not exist, SA8000 requires that management

"shall facilitate parallel means of independent and free association."

SA8000 aims to increase awareness of basic human rights.

How far down the supply chain does a facility need to go before attaining a certificate to SA8000?

The SA8000 standard encourages companies to use the leverage of their business to ensure that their suppliers conform to SA8000. It is important to note that certification is facility specific. A certificate of compliance with SA8000 can only be issued once a full SA audit has taken place and compliance demonstrated. SA8000 requires each facility to

"establish and maintain appropriate procedures to evaluate and select suppliers based on their ability to meet with requirements of this standard."

The facility also needs to

"maintain appropriate records of suppliers' commitment to social accountability, including, but not limited to, the suppliers' written commitment to:

a. conform to all requirements of this standard

b. participate in the company's monitoring activities as requested

c. promptly remediate any nonconformance identified against the requirements of this standard

d. promptly and completely inform the company of any and all relevant business relationship(s) with other suppliers and subcontractor(s).

The company shall maintain reasonable evidence that the requirements of this standard are being met by suppliers and subcontractors."

How does SA8000 compare to other initiatives to promote social standards?

There are numerous initiatives that promote workers' rights in both the US and in Europe. There are signs of a growing convergence among standards, both in terms of content and in regard to management systems.

In the USA, major initiatives include: the Fair Labor Association and the Worldwide Responsible Apparel Production program.

The Fair Labor Association (FLA)

In 1996, President Clinton convened the Apparel Industry Partnership to address the issue of workers' rights. The result of the negotiations is the Fair Labor Association, a non-profit organization that intends to accredit independent monitors to inspect factories. The FLA also plans to deal with complaints from interested parties. The following companies are participating in the FLA: Nike, Reebok, Philips van Heusen, and Liz Claiborne, among others. **While NGOs and unions participated in the drafting of the Fair Labor Charter, unions have since withdrawn their support.**

The FLA approach differs from SA8000 in eight important ways

- SA8000 is a global system, whereas FLA is a US initiative.

- SA8000 is not industry-sector specific, whereas the FLA is only for the apparel and footwear industries.

- FLA's Workplace Code of Conduct does not require companies to pay a "living wage." While both the FLA's Workplace Code of Conduct and SA8000 guarantee the right of workers to organize, only SA8000 sets a requirement for countries in which the right to organize is restricted by law. In these countries, companies shall facilitate parallel means of organizing. SA8000 is fully operational now; but the FLA has a three-year phase-in period before it becomes operational, which is designed to allow for adequate time for the FLA to assess whether companies are making a good faith effort to promote workers' rights.

- The FLA will determine which factories should be monitored, based on risk analysis and company recommendation. As a result, 85 per-cent of applicable facilities will not be monitored in a given year.[23]

- Over-time must always be remunerated at a premium rate under SA8000, whereas under the FLA Code premium rates are mandated only in countries that have legislation requiring it.

- The FLA certifies global *companies*, not factories, as SA8000 does.

- The FLA accreditation system is not ISO compliant whereas the SA8000 model is.

The Worldwide Responsible Apparel Production (WRAP)

WRAP is a voluntary program which provides guidelines for monitoring and intends to develop a certification system. An industry-wide initiative led by the American Apparel Manufacturing Association.

WRAP differs from SA8000 in that it is a US program focused on a single industry, whereas SA8000 is both global and multi-industry. WRAP also encompasses issues that are not part of SA8000, such as drug interdiction, environment, and customs compliance.[24] Another major difference is that trade unions and NGOs are not part of the WRAP Certification Board, but are part of SAI's Advisory Board. Another key difference involves the definition of compliance to the standard. In many areas, the WRAP standard requires only compliance with national laws, whereas SA8000 uses national legislation as a starting point.

The major European initiatives to address workers' rights include the Ethical Trading Initiative and Clean Clothes Campaign. AccountAbility 1000 will be addressed in Chapter 7 on Communicating about SA8000.

Ethical Trading Initiative (ETI)

This is a UK initiative which seeks to improve working conditions around the world by creating a forum for debate on socially responsible practice for companies sourcing in the developing world. The ETI is tri-partite, consisting of groups from three sectors: companies, NGOs, and unions. The ETI base code closely resembles SA8000, as both are based on ILO conventions. Funded by the UK government's Department for International Development and the private sector, the ETI is conducting several pilot audits determine best practices in monitoring. ETI is interested in sharing the lessons learned from various different approaches to monitoring. Among the participating companies are: C&A, Sainsbury's, and the Co-operative Wholesale Society, along with NGOs such as Save the Children and the FairTrade Foundation.

Key differences between ETI and SA8000 include the following: SA8000 is global, whereas ETI consists primarily of UK companies, with one major company headquartered in the USA, and some internationally-focused NGOs and trade unions. ETI promotes a comparative analysis of different approaches to promoting workers' rights, whereas SA8000 is an operational system for accredited certification. Both ETI and SA8000 have consulted with a wide range of NGOs and unions around the world.

Clean Clothes Campaign (CCC)

This is a European-wide voluntary initiative with branches in Austria, Belgium, France, Germany, Italy, The Netherlands, Spain, Sweden, and Switzerland. CCC has developed a code of conduct which also closely resembles SA8000, as it too is based on ILO conventions. CCC seeks to create national tri-partite bodies that decide whether to certify a company. These tri-partite groups would include unions, NGOs, and companies who jointly review information from the auditors before deciding whether to certify a facility.

The CCC focuses exclusively on the garment industry. One major difference between CCC and other initiatives is that the CCC does not include companies in its governance body, only NGOs and unions. Another difference between SA8000 and CCC is that CCC supports the exclusive use of unannounced visits by auditors. A proposal made by the Swedish CCC raised the possibility that the CCC and SA8000 could be complementary if a company sought to meet the requirements of both initiatives, hired a firm accredited by SAI to verify and then had the audit report reviewed by a tri-partite national body. CCC reviewed and commented extensively during the development of SA8000.

Figure 1.2 ■ A comparison of key initiatives (both planned and operational)[25]

	Scope	Industry focus	Distinctive aspects of content	Objective
SA8000	Global	Multi-industry management systems	Living wage	Develop accreditation and certification procedure for facilities
FLA	USA*	Apparel Footwear		Develop accreditation/label for global companies
WRAP	USA*	Apparel	Environment customs, drug interdiction	Factory certification
ETI	UK**	Multi-industry	Living wage	Share learning; develop methodology
CCC	European	Garment retail	Living wage	Develop tri-partite certification

*   Factories and suppliers are located all over the world, but companies signing on to the proposal have headquarters in the US.

** Factories and suppliers are located all over the world, but companies signing on to the proposal have headquarters in the UK.

Chapter 2 presents case studies on some of the most well-known companies adopting SA8000. One of the key messages from the case studies is how widely the strategies differ for implementing SA8000. Likewise, the lessons learned by one company may not be consistent with lessons learned by other companies, as there are regional and sectoral differences. On the other hand, there is convergence on the need to take action and the motivations for adopting SA8000.

2
Lessons learned from SA8000 leaders

Companies around the world are working within the framework of SA8000. Among these companies are the signatory members listed in Fig. 2.1.

Together, these companies have annual revenues of $106 billion. Commitment to SA8000 comes not only from the private sector, but also from governments and multilateral agencies. The UN Office for Project Services (UNOPS) has also become an SA8000 member. This chapter contains case studies of several of these companies and the lessons they have learned about implementation of social standards.

There are some 60 companies that are certified to SA8000 but are not SA8000 members, including:

- Co-op Italia with headquarters in Italy
- De Nadai Alimentacão with headquarters in Brazil
- L.E. Jones Company with headquarters in the USA
- WE Europe with headquarters in the Netherlands.

In addition, there are companies that are not members or certified but are asking their suppliers to become certified, including: Difrax whose headquarters are in The Netherlands; and Kesko whose headquarters are in Finland.

Figure 2.1 ■ Signatory members of SA8000

Name	HQ country	Industry	Annual gross revenues
Amana	Switzerland	Apparel – Amana's LINK Fair Trade Label is a clothing line sold in Europe made by suppliers in the developing world who receive support from Amana to meet SA8000	Less than $25 million
Avon Products	USA	Cosmetics	$5 billion
Cutter & Buck	USA	Apparel – a fast growing leader in golf apparel	$150 million
Dole Food Products	USA	Food – world's No. 1 producer of fresh fruits and vegetables	$5 billion
Eileen Fisher	USA	Apparel – private maker of women's clothing line sold through its own stores and major department stores	$25–100 million
Otto Versand	Germany	Mail order – largest catalog retailer in the world	$24 billion
Promodes (subsidiary of Carrefour)	France	Retail – Carrefour operates hypermarkets and is the second largest retailer in the world	$59 billion
Toys "R" Us	USA	Toys – largest toy retailer in the world	$12 billion
United Nations Office of Project Services	USA	The UN's project management and procurement agency	$500 million
		Total	$106 billion

■ Case study Avon Products

"Cheap labor is not cheap, it's expensive in terms of human lives."

Fitz Hilaire, Director of Global Supplier Development, Avon[1]

Founded in 1886, Avon was one of the first companies to offer women career opportunities, 34 years before women were able to vote in the USA. The company's central focus has always been women, from its employees to its customers. Hence, protecting the company's workers, who are generally women, was of paramount concern. Avon sells cosmetics, jewelry, gift items, clothing, CDs, books, and videos. In 1999, the company had $5.2 billion in sales, with 2.8 million direct representatives. The company seeks to be both grassroots and global, marketing its products in 135 countries.

Avon has played a leadership role in developing and promoting SA8000. The company's goal is to have its own factories compliant with SA8000 and all of its suppliers certified to SA8000. Each year, Avon buys $1 billion in goods; the company seeks to reinforce its values through its sourcing policy.

Avon began its work on human rights by developing its own code of conduct: Avon Global Ethics. It soon became clear that it was impossible to have two standards in the company: Avon Global Ethics and SA8000. As a result, Avon adopted SA8000 as the company's code. Implementation began by developing step-by-step practical guidelines for manufacturing sites. Avon has developed software for monitoring its supply chain.

Each facility has had minor issues that need to be addressed before achieving certification. **After implementing SA8000, one of Avon's facilities in upstate New York remarked "had we known how useful a human resources tool SA8000 is, we would have sought certification anyway, even without prompting from headquarters."**[2]

According to Robert Cowling, Vice President of Global Sourcing at Avon:

"SA8000 is good for workers, customers, and communities."[3]

Cowling believes that in order to implement SA8000, it is necessary to have the following.

Leadership is necessary to promote social goals within a company. In the case of Avon, Fitz Hilaire provided the passionate commitment that drove the implementation of SA8000 as chair of the SA8000 Advisory Board. Former CEOs Jim Preston and Charles Perrin also played a pivotal role. Glen Clark of the Avon Foundation initiated Avon's commitment to SA8000.

Education is necessary as a mechanism for sharing the vision throughout the organization and with suppliers. It is crucial for implementation of the standard that the benefits of SA8000 are clearly understood and that the company's values are communicated throughout the supply chain. The program needs to reach the regional and local levels of the company. Assigning people in each region is critical for success. Avon has assigned 20 employees as monitors who develop timelines and goals, manage the database of suppliers, track progress, and flag problem areas, while sharing the vision of SA8000 at the local level. Their greatest achievement so far has been to promote awareness of and commitment to SA8000 in the 135 countries where Avon operates.

Local involvement is critical, as buy-in is needed at all levels.

Clear goals: the monitors tell suppliers that to be a world-class supplier or manufacturing factory for Avon, SA8000 certification is necessary.

Reports of progress – communication is essential for continued commitment to SA8000.

lessons learned by Avon

It is imperative that if the monitoring is to be effective there must be an active database for measuring the results of the effort. An interactive database where all contributors can view the ongoing progress is essential for the success and transparency of the program. Avon has decided to phase in the certification of its suppliers starting with the areas that are most likely to be high risk to the normal supplier base, giving high priority to suppliers in apparel, gifts, jewelry, and toys.

Case study Co-op Italia

Co-op Italia is the largest supermarket chain in Italy, with 1200 points of sale and more than 30 hypermarkets, controlling 7 percent of the Italian market. The company has 36,000 employees and over 3 million members throughout Italy. Co-op Italia sells a wide range of products, from food to clothing and toys. The company is part of Lega-Coop and benefits from the strong position of the Co-op movement in Italy.

SA8000 helps Co-op Italia to earn the trust of consumers and to avert business risks. Risks are very high in the food industry. Alessandra Vacarri (a consultant to Co-op Italia on social and ethical issues) gives the following example of the nature of these risks. Mad cow disease caused European food retailers to lose as much as 50 percent in market share on average. Co-op Italia lost only 3 percent because they had developed policies and procedures to address food safety concerns.

The SA8000 standard is being applied to 230 suppliers of their private label food program. **The company reports that 99 percent of their suppliers want to work with the SA8000 system.**[4] In 2000, Co-op Italia sent SA8000 to non-food suppliers and to service suppliers. It took two months to create the database system, including the development of checklists and data-entry.

All employees have received SA8000 training. The company has hired two full-time staff to review checklists from suppliers and to develop a database. Training is provided for quality inspectors, buyers, and marketing and trademark staff.

In the first year (1999), Co-op Italia audited a sample of 25 of its suppliers that are part of the more critical supply chains, and several of their subcontractors through external certification audits. The key product lines chosen include tomatoes, fruit, and frozen fish. The tomato processing operations produce only for Co-op Italia. Critical suppliers are so defined by the kind of product and the geographical location where they are produced.

Co-op Italia gave an example of a small bakery having difficulty in requiring a very large company, which produced flour, to complete the checklist. The bakery simply did not have the leverage.

📖 lessons learned by Co-op Italia

1. Small suppliers have difficulties convincing their large company suppliers to provide them with checklists.
2. All suppliers need to improve their management systems.

Case study Dole Food Company, Inc.

Dole Food Company, INC., with 1999 revenues of $5.1 billion, is the world's largest producer and marketer of fresh fruit, vegetables, and fresh-cut flowers and markets a growing line of packaged foods. With operations in over 90 countries, the company employs more than 53,000 people in a variety of operations, including farming, manufacturing, food processing, research, marketing and sales, and distribution. Dole owns its own fleet of ships.

Dole was an early participant in the effort to develop and implement the SA8000 standard. The company hosted two pilot site assessments to test the application of SA8000 in the agricultural sector, and has conducted several additional internal audits throughout its worldwide operations. In June 2000, Dole announced the certification to SA8000 of

Pascual Hermanos, a Dole subsidiary, which is the largest fruit and vegetable operation in Spain. Pascual employs 3000 people in 11 growing, processing, and packing sites. In recognition of having the first agricultural operation in the world certified to SA8000, Social Accountability International awarded Dole the Ethical Workplace Award at the annual CEP Corporate Conscience Awards Dinner in New York City in June 2000.

There are several issues that Dole is addressing as part of its social accountability program. These include working hours and health and safety issues, although probably the most significant issue that the company faces is its relationship to suppliers – in particular, the small farmers that supply Dole with produce. The number of suppliers from which Dole sources is in the thousands, and often these suppliers are small family farmers, some of whom, without assistance, would have difficulty understanding and carrying out the procedures necessary to adequately protect and maintain health and safety requirements. To provide this assistance, Dole has implemented a program within the context of its environmental management systems worldwide to offer technical, educational, and often financial assistance to suppliers, to help bring them up to the Dole standard of environmental and social responsibility.

Dole currently has a policy that supports the principles of social accountability, and addresses environmental and anti-corruption issues as well. An updated policy, currently under consideration, will address more precisely the issues raised in SA8000 and the principles outlined in the United Nation's Global Compact Initiative[5] among others.

According to Sharon Hayes of Dole,

"The company is proud of its record on social accountability. It was recently named among the top ten most socially accountable companies by the Council on Economic Priorities in its book, Shopping For A Better World. *The company hopes to have other certifications to SA8000 to report in 2001 and beyond."[6]*

📖 lessons learned by Dole

Among the lessons learned in Dole's SA8000 initiative is that a social accountability system is easier to install when it is built on a foundation of experience with systems already in place, such as ISO14001. It is also necessary to have top-level support for the effort throughout the company, and it is valuable to have recognition programs, both internal and external, for a company's social responsibility efforts.

▧ Case study Eileen Fisher

Eileen Fisher is an American women's clothing manufacturer and retailer, with 1999 sales of $90 million. The product is distributed through 21 Eileen Fisher retail and outlet stores in the USA, as well as department stores and independent boutiques. It has suppliers in New York and in China, but does not own or operate any of its manufacturing facilities. Eileen Fisher was one of the very first companies to participate in the development of SA8000. David Zwiebel, then of Eileen Fisher, played a key role in developing and promoting SA8000.

The company's commitment to social issues is a long-standing tradition. Eileen Fisher supports a number of women's causes through charitable donations and volunteerism; it is known for a corporate culture emphasizing lifestyle and family.

Amy Hall, Manager of Social Accountability at Eileen Fisher (EF), sees the relationship between suppliers and the company evolving. Price, quality, speed, and organization are no longer the only aspects of a good supplier. In order for there to be a successful supplier relationship, there must also be:

- shared business values
- mutual trust
- creative problem-solving.

Shared business values can be seen in the way the company places an emphasis on the individual, seeking to treat suppliers fairly. For example,

"it's important to give suppliers adequate lead time. We can't give them a huge order on a Friday and expect that it will be completed by Monday morning."[7]

In order to develop mutual trust, the supplier and EF must share information openly and use that information responsibly.

"Creative problem-solving is required if we, together with our suppliers, are to help change 100 years of garment industry tradition."[8]

Eileen Fisher is seeking to become SA8000 certified and to encourage its suppliers to become certified as well. The company has staff dedicated to working with suppliers to improve social conditions at supplier factories. Over the course of several years, staff have visited 25 factories, the majority of them in New York City. Among the most pervasive problems they've found are wage and hour violations and these are the most difficult to identify without the co-operation of the factories themselves. It has taken a full year for suppliers and their workers to come forward with information, such as unreported cash payments or hidden over-time hours. Only when this information is known can the company and its suppliers begin to work together to find reasonable solutions that can be achieved within a specific timeframe.

As part of its partnership approach to its relationships with suppliers, EF has developed various mechanisms for providing support. Where warranted, the company provides both technical and financial assistance. It also recognizes the importance of maintaining a steady workflow with its core contractors – a seemingly simple concept that today's trend-conscious companies find challenging to meet.

lessons learned by Eileen Fisher

1. Implementing SA8000 takes time, especially if the factory has no prior experience with codes of conduct. This process cannot be rushed.

2. "We, as a company, need to follow the standard too. How can we ask our vendors to comply without first 'stepping up to bat'?"[9]

3. It is more difficult for small suppliers to implement SA8000, as they often have a small staff and no computers to maintain records. (Note: Not all companies would agree with this, as big companies often face additional barriers. In addition, while computers make managing the SA8000 system easier, they are not essential.)

Visiting suppliers to address social issues has led Eileen Fisher to offer health care to workers at its non-union core US contractors. (Core contractors are those that maintain a steady workload of at least 90 percent Eileen Fisher product.) In one factory, Eileen Fisher pays a per-garment surcharge for every garment produced, thereby helping the factory to afford basic health care (through a major Health Maintenance Organization (HMO)[10] and a New York State healthcare program) for every worker who wants it. This surcharge is tracked separately to ensure that the funds are being used for the stated purpose. In time, this cost will be absorbed into the regular pricing structure of the garments.

To date, only one supplier has signed up for this health care program. Others are considering it, pending the outcome of the pilot program. For each participating supplier, the amount of the surcharge could vary, depending on the average number of garments produced by the factory, their monthly overhead expenses, and the number of full-time workers who would qualify for health insurance.

While this is only a pilot program, it has shown promising results after six months. Several workers have taken advantage of their new health care plan, using it not only for emergency purposes but also for preventive care. Perhaps the biggest hurdle has been in the processing of paperwork, to which they are not accustomed. Above all, this program has enabled the workers to get off welfare-provided services and into mainstream American society.

■ Case study Kesko

Kesko is the largest wholesale retail group in Finland, with sales of 6.5 billion Euros in 1999. The company and the 1800 member retailers run several retail chains, carrying a variety of products, including food, building supplies, clothing, home furnishings, and phones. Kesko also has an agriculture division. The company has 42,000 suppliers producing for seven product groups. Kesko imports from 70 countries. In some cases, products are purchased through buying organizations such as AMS, Viking Fruit, Euromateriaux, Intersport, and others. Kesko's goal is to be "the best company in Scandinavia"; as such it is concerned with its social responsibility. In addition to working within the SA8000 system, Kesko has made an "ethical trading initiative" in Finland, in order to produce common ethical principles for all companies importing from the developing world. The Finnish Foreign Ministry participates in this initiative. Kesko is also working with UNICEF to eliminate child labor in Bhiwandi, the center of the looming industry in the state of Maharashtra, India.

Since the 1980s, Kesko has had a policy prohibiting its buyers from purchasing goods made with child labor, making it one of the first companies to develop such a policy. Kesko is implementing SA8000 because it seeks to be proactive. Kesko executives presented SA8000 to the Board of Directors, who then approved the standard to be used as Kesko's basic tool in ethical quality control. In April 2000, Kesko launched a code of conduct based on SA8000, which also includes a section on anti-corruption measures. Kesko now sends their questionnaire on social accountability, which includes a section on anti-corruption measures, to every one of their suppliers in the developing world and motivates the suppliers through personal conversations to start co-operating with certification bodies and to apply for certification. **SA8000-certified suppliers will be favored in purchasing, and Kesko does not start commercial relations with new suppliers without having them pre-audited first as part of its risk analysis.** Kesko also initiated a two-day training course on SA8000, organized by SAI.

Kesko plans to work with its purchasing organizations on SA8000. On a bilateral basis, Kesko has already agreed with ICA (food) and Åhlens (non-food) of Sweden that SA8000 will be the basis of their joint purchasing operations in the Far East.

Kesko hopes to inform consumers about its commitment to SA8000 by giving store personnel basic information about the standard and by writing about SA8000 in their customer magazine which, with 1.2 million copies, goes to half of the households in Finland. Kesko also plans to integrate SA8000 with both ISO14000 and ISO9000. A greater number of their suppliers are certified to ISO9000 than to ISO14000, especially in the food industry. The non-food industry companies are normally smaller than the food suppliers and not yet as advanced in using standards. In many cases, it seems sensible for the suppliers to start implementing both the quality management system and the social accountability system simultaneously, as the total costs will then be lower. The costs are a problem that has to be overcome. Kesko is not going to finance the implementation of SA8000 at the supplier level, reasoning that the certificate benefits all customers, not only Kesko.

Case study Otto Versand

Otto Versand is the world's largest catalog company, with 83 subsidiaries in 23 countries, including the USA, the UK, and Asia. The product range is varied, from garments to rugs. In 1999–2000, the Otto Trading Group had a turnover of 40.1 billion Euros and employed 74,000 people. There are 15 employees who focus exclusively on environmental issues; the company has a tradition of caring about sustainable issues, offering a line of socially-responsible products, such as clothing made from organic cotton and Rugmark carpets.[11]

Otto seeks to develop a relationship with its suppliers based on co-operation and partnership. The company does not seek to play the game "cops and robbers," in which the buyer creates an atmosphere of distrust. Otto's approach is to treat suppliers as partners. Thus, they announce the dates when audits will occur as a means of fostering trust. They also raise suppliers' willingness to co-operate by combining quality, environmental, and social audits. The co-operation principle has proven its worth, as it has led to a positive reaction from suppliers, while fostering a high degree of openness. Suppliers are taking greater care to choose better subcontractors. Auditors report that there is marked improvement in overall social performance when they visit a factory for the second time.[12]

> THE CO-OPERATION PRINCIPLE HAS PROVEN ITS WORTH, AS IT HAS LED TO A POSITIVE REACTION FROM SUPPLIERS, WHILE FOSTERING A HIGH DEGREE OF OPENNESS

Over the course of the past few years, Otto has organized workshops for suppliers, meetings with both governmental and non-governmental organizations, and workshops for their own staff. The company's implementation strategy is to provide social responsibility training for its quality auditors. These workshops focus on increasing awareness that social responsibility is not about protectionism. Otto Versand explains the sustainability principle, interprets its code of conduct, and provides background on the labor laws and social policies in the country in which the auditors work. The company also introduces auditors to the SAI Guidance Document for SA8000. The workshop will also help the suppliers to implement SA8000 and to get ready for certification in the shortest possible time-frame.

Otto Versand has conducted 300 audits in its major import markets: Turkey, the Philippines, South Korea, Indonesia, Vietnam, India, Thailand, and China. All visits were announced in advance and no sanctions were given without allowing the supplier adequate time to take corrective action.

In many countries, auditors have found a discrepancy between the minimum wage and a living wage. The company considers this to be a structural problem that will require significant involvement from many bodies, including governments, NGOs, and multilateral agencies such as the World Bank. According to Achim Lohrie, Director of Strategy for Environment and Social Policy at Otto Versand,

"it is necessary to raise the debate to a political level, as buyers and their suppliers cannot solve the issue alone."[13]

In the interim, Otto Versand requires their suppliers to gradually phase in a living wage.

Otto Versand's research yielded an interesting lesson.

📖 lessons learned by Otto Versand

"There is a connection between the size or structure of the audited company and its social performance. The smaller the business, the worse its social performance."[14] SA8000 imposes requirements on companies to develop management systems, making it difficult for small companies which lack any pre-existing management systems. Thus it is easier for large and medium-sized companies to attain SA8000.

According to Otto's experience, these small companies lack both management structures and understanding of management systems and an infrastructure to meet procedural requirements.

The challenge will be to encourage companies sourcing worldwide to provide training and advice to suppliers, as well as internal auditing, combined with quality and environmental audits. In other words, "to help suppliers to help themselves."[15]

📖 lessons learned by Otto Versand

1. It is essential to have both male and female auditors.
2. It is important to develop industry-specific risk factors in the areas of health and safety.
3. No supplier was found to be ready for certification without some preparation.
4. It's important to be able to negotiate with suppliers.
5. Otto Versand gives suppliers two or three chances before deciding to drop them.
6. In dealing with the worst sub-suppliers, it's good to enforce the code through the main supplier.
7. Implementation is a step-by-step process. The first step should be the full implementation of legal requirements which will already be a task for many suppliers and their sub-

suppliers.[16] The second step is implementation of management systems, gaining understanding of the value of those systems with regard to all sustainability issues, economic prosperity, and social responsibility.

Otto Versand promotes SA8000 throughout the German retail industry, aware that if more retailers require SA8000 of their suppliers, the SA8000 certificate will become more widespread. They are also involved with co-operative activities with several development agencies and industry associations, seeking to improve working conditions.

Case study Promodes

Promodes is a French distribution group, operating supermarkets, hyper-markets, and convenience stores throughout France, Spain, Italy, Portugal, and Belgium, as well as in Asia and South America. In 1999, Carrefour acquired Promodes, uniting France's two biggest retailers. The result is Europe's biggest retail chain and the second largest in the world, with 9400 stores in 27 countries, a labor force of 340,000 and a turnover of 52 billion Euros. At the time of publication, there was intense discussion as to whether Carrefour would work within the SA8000 system.

Towards the end of 1996, Promodes decided to introduce social issues to its suppliers of non-food products, including toys, footwear, and textiles. They formed a small task group and began to draft a code of conduct. While drafting their own company code, Promodes became aware of SA8000. With suppliers in 20 countries, Promodes realized that it would be easier and far more credible to adopt a global code rather than an internal code.

At the end of 1998, the company began its implementation of SA8000 by sending the standard to 150 suppliers in the Asia-Pacific region, Morocco and Tunisia, all in non-food sectors. A significant percentage of the non-food imports is sourced from the Asia-Pacific Rim.

The standard was followed by a questionnaire based on SA8000. An external inspection firm contacted the suppliers and received replies. A sample of 30 suppliers was also audited to provide the company with a better understanding of what was happening and what could realistically be improved. Promodes is in the process of defining what social account-ability means for the company. Another major task is developing training programs for buyers. Promodes experienced difficulties in locating the actual production and subcontracting facilities of goods being sourced.

Case study Toys "R" Us

Toys "R" Us is the largest toy retailer in the world. The company does not own any manufacturing sites, but sources all of its products. The company operates 1585 stores worldwide with 711 toy stores in the USA, 492 international toy stores, 198 Kids "R" Us clothing stores, 144 Babies "R" Us stores, and 40 Imaginarium stores. The company also sells merchandise through its Internet sites at toysrus.com, babriesrus.com, and imaginarium.com.

The company employs over 50,000 workers worldwide. It sources product from over 30 different countries and has over 3000 product suppliers. The majority of its toy products are manufactured by suppliers located in China. Throughout its various operations the company stocks tens of thousands of different products.

Founded in 1948, Toys "R" Us established its reputation of sound business relationships and partnerships with its suppliers – a practice that it still continues today. In 1995, the issues of social accountability in the workplace received national public exposure. From sub-standard work conditions to employment of underage workers, retailers such as Toys "R" Us have come under increasing public pressure to ensure that their merchandise is produced in factories that maintain and promote acceptable workplace standards. Recognizing its obligation as a retailer of children's products and that of a global corporate citizen, the company has assumed a prominent role in advocating social accountability. The company's role in promoting the rights of workers is evidenced by its representation on the Board of Directors of Social Accountability International (SAI), the Board of Directors of SAI's Governing Board, the Accreditation Review Panel of SAI, and the Advisory Board of SAI. The company is a member of SA8000 and a sponsor of SAI Conferences on Strategic Management of Global Workplace Social Accountability.

In 1997 the company developed and distributed its Code of Conduct for Suppliers program to all of its suppliers. In that same year, the company was recognized by SAI as a recipient of its Global Corporate Conscience Award.

In 1999, the company adopted SA8000. Tom De Luca of Toys "R" Us believes SA8000 is the best initiative for its businesses. Its cross-industry application goes beyond the company's traditional toy business and can be applied to the company's other strategic product categories. SA8000, a collaborative effort by several cross-industry global enterprises, government agencies, and non-government representatives should, once fully adopted by suppliers, permit organizations like Toys "R" Us to rely on the certification process in lieu of performing in-house compliance reviews of suppliers.

However, Toys "R" Us faces significant challenges in implementing SA8000. The first challenge is that a majority of its products are sourced from China, where law restricts freedom of association. Second, many product lines have very deep supply chains, with some toys having many additional suppliers producing components.

Recently, the toy industry launched its own initiative with the ICTI Code of Business Practices, a joint effort by the Toy Manufacturers of America (TMA) and the Toy Industries of Europe. Similar in many ways to SAI's SA8000, the ICTI initiative is establishing an independent auditing organization to certify factories for compliance. While SA8000 is already operational in the workplace, with many certifications already completed, the toy industry code is still under development. However, many toy factories have taken a "wait-and-see" attitude towards engagement, pending release of the finished product from the toy industry.

More recently, the US Customs Service issued a new customs advisory announcing efforts in preventing the importation into the USA of merchandise produced in whole or in part with prison labor, forced labor, or indentured labor including forced or indentured child labor under penal sanctions under the provisions of the Tariff Act of 1930. The advisory describes the types of working conditions that may, in the view of the US Customs Service, signal the presence of forced or indentured child labor. The advisory assists manufacturers, retailers, importers, and other businesses involved in importing merchandise from foreign countries, providing guidance for compliance with US Federal law prohibiting the importation into the USA of goods produced under these conditions.

This new US Customs Advisory should heighten the awareness level of responsibility to those engaged in the production, exportation, and importation of products into the USA, and certainly bring the issue of child labor abuses to the forefront of those involved in promoting social accountability around the world.

Case study WE Europe

With 280 stores in six countries, WE Europe is a major European retailer of men's, women's, and children's clothing. WE Europe is also the second biggest shareholder of Saks Fifth Avenue. A privately-held company, WE Europe's mission is to be the best retailer in Western Europe – "in fashion, quality, prices, publicity, and social accountability."[17]

In 1998, the company began to receive between eight and ten letters per week from concerned consumers worried about whether children were involved in manufacturing clothing for WE Europe. These letters began to arrive on the desk of Mr Frits Nagel, Purchase Controller. According to Mr Nagel, WE Europe wanted

"to respect the right of customers to know how our products are made."

Mr Nagel believes that customers are willing to buy more if they can be certain that their clothing is made in a socially-responsible manner. According to a presentation by Mr Nagel, 60 percent of consumers in The Netherlands are interested in the conditions in which products are made.

One of the key trends that influenced WE Europe is the changing nature of jurisprudence, which now allows Europeans to be tried in Europe for crimes committed abroad. This trend suggests that it may be possible to hold European managers accountable for the abusive conditions under which their products are made overseas.

In considering the company's strategy, Mr Nagel proposed that a global social code was necessary to promote higher standards throughout the world. The Board of Directors made the decision to adopt SA8000. Mr Nagel compares SA8000 to the Woolmark, which guarantees that a product is 100 percent wool and which is adopted all over the world, to ISO90002 and ISO14002. Without a globally-accepted norm, suppliers rejected by WE Europe for poor social conditions would simply manufacture for WE's competitors at a lower price. In the long term, the buyers have to look for alternative manufacturers when managers are not willing or not in a position to apply for SA8000 certification.

CUSTOMERS ARE WILLING TO BUY MORE IF THEY CAN BE CERTAIN THAT THEIR CLOTHING IS MADE IN A SOCIALLY-RESPONSIBLE MANNER

After receiving approval and funding from its Board of Directors, WE Europe decided to ask their suppliers to conform to SA8000.

"But then a very smart Chinese supplier asked if WE Europe was also going to implement SA8000,"

reports Mr Nagel. So WE Europe decided to also implement SA8000 at its headquarters in The Netherlands. What obstacles did the company face in implementing SA8000 in its own headquarters? A pre-audit by a major certification firm reveals that the company will need to develop a management system to address health and safety concerns, to clear emergency doors, and to create a system of regular fire-drills.

WE Europe expects to receive certification by early 2001. In two years, WE Europe expects that two-thirds of its suppliers will become SA8000 certified. One hundred percent compliance will be difficult, as high fashion dictates new materials and trends which often require a supplier base which is in constant change. WE Europe began the implementation process by reviewing which suppliers they will be working with in the next six years, and which suppliers had been important to the company in previous years. Simultaneously, the company began to develop a code of conduct which mirrors SA8000, but adds two additional areas: the use of chemicals and the environment.

WE Europe code

Use of chemicals

The contractor will avoid the use of the following chemicals that can seriously harm the health of the employees and the consumers:

A. forbidden carcinogenic aromatic amines in concentrations higher than 30 mg/Kg

B. formaldehyde in concentration higher than 100 ppm for garments with direct skin contact and 300 ppm for garments without direct skin contact

C. nickel for all metal accessories

D. cadmium

E. PCP.

The environment

The contractor certifies that he will comply with all applicable environmental laws and regulations in the country of production and he will study the continuous improvements in process and programs in order to reduce the impact on the environment.[18]

The next step involved communicating the importance of the code to WE Europe's own employees. This was done through a series of lectures to product buyers. The code was put on the Internet and reported on in the press.

According to Frits Nagel,

"SA8000 will not increase costs to the consumer. Small suppliers may need to have some assistance in order to come into compliance with SA8000."[19]

Suppliers have already reported benefits associated with the implementation of SA8000, including increased productivity and enhanced worker morale.[20]

Chapter 3 breaks down the SA8000 code into each of its provisions or issue areas. This chapter contains key definitions, along with all of the provisions of SA8000 in italics. For some issue areas, an overview is provided. Readers are advised to read this chapter in conjunction with the *SA8000 Guidance Document* which contains excellent background on many issues. At the end of each issue area, there are links to other parts of SA8000. These links are important, as they show the inter-relatedness of the sections of the standard. Most of the sections inter-connect, meaning that if a facility faces problems in one area, problems can arise in related areas. Likewise, a management system that takes into account one issue, can have an unexpected link to another issue area as well.

3

A framework for understanding SA8000

Based on internationally agreed principles, **SA8000 is based on a premise that human rights are a global concept, that do not vary from country to country.** Likewise, the founders of SA8000 believe that human rights and trade are not mutually exclusive. Workers' rights – like human rights – are not a new concept. The struggle to promote better working conditions has been underway for centuries, with the International Labour Organization (ILO) serving as a focal point for several decades. This chapter begins with a brief history of the ILO, its purpose and scope.

The International Labour Organization

The International Labour Organization (ILO) was established in 1919 to promote social justice and internationally recognized human and labor rights. The ILO is the only United Nations body with a tri-partite structure, giving voice to unions, governments, and employers' organizations (which represent companies). The ILO is one of only two UN agencies to have received the Nobel Peace Prize.

The ILO formulates labor standards through conventions and recommendations which set minimum standards. These are agreed upon by national governments, unions, and employers' organizations. SA8000 is based on conventions of the ILO, the UN Declaration of Human Rights, and the UN Convention on the Rights of the Child. It is important to emphasize that the mandate of the ILO is to set standards for countries. If the ILO has already stipulated minimum standards, why is SA8000 necessary? ILO conventions are ratified by countries, which commit to ensuring that their domestic legislation conforms to their obligations under the conventions. SA8000, by contrast, is a standard for implementation at the facility level, with a certificate for compliance.

SA8000 provides an auditable framework for companies. It is written in short, clear terms designed for managers to implement, rather than a long, complex document designed for diplomats and legislators to use as a basis for the formulation of laws.

Issues addressed by SA8000

The following section provides a framework on working conditions with background on each major section of SA8000. The reader is strongly encouraged to refer to the *SA8000 Guidance Document* for an overview of major issues.

Each section of SA8000 is inherently linked to other aspects of the standard. These links are explored at the end of each section and provide a useful angle for companies implementing the standard.

Child labor

SA8000 definitions

Child: any person less than 15 years of age, unless local minimum age law stipulates a higher age for work or mandatory schooling, in which case the higher age would apply. If, however, local minimum age law is set at 14 years of age in accordance with developing-country exceptions under ILO Convention 138, the lower age will apply.

Child labor: any work by a child younger than the age(s) specified in the above definition of a child, except as provided for by ILO Recommendation 146.

Remediation of children: all necessary support and actions to ensure the safety, health, education, and development of children who have been subjected to child labor, as defined above, and are dismissed.

Young worker: any worker over the age of a child as defined above and under the age of 18.

SA8000 provisions

SA8000 1.1 *The company shall not engage in or support the use of child labor as defined above;*

SA8000 1.2 *The company shall establish, document, maintain, and effectively communicate to personnel and other interested parties policies and procedures for remediation of children found to be working in situations which fit the definition of child labor above, and shall provide adequate support to enable such children to attend and remain in school until no longer a child as defined above.*

SA8000 1.3 *The company shall establish, document, maintain, and effectively communicate to personnel and other interested parties policies and procedures for promotion of education for children covered under ILO Recommendation 146 and young workers who are subject to local compulsory education laws or are attending school, including means to ensure that no such child or young worker is employed during school hours and that combined hours of daily transportation (to and from work and school), school, and work time does not exceed 10 hours per day.*

SA8000 1.4 *The company shall not expose children or young workers to situations in or outside the workplace that are hazardous, unsafe, or unhealthy.*

Overview

The International Labour Organization estimates that there are at least 250 million children between the ages of 5 and 14 who work.[1] Approximately 150 million of these children work full time and/or under hazardous conditions. It is difficult to give a precise estimate, as child labor, like other illegal activities, is not something which employers report. Of the 250 million child workers, the majority are in Asia (61 percent), followed by Africa (32 percent), and then by Latin America (7 percent).[2]

CHILD LABOR IS A VERY COMPLEX ISSUE WHICH NEEDS TO BE ADDRESSED BY A WIDE RANGE OF PARTIES, INCLUDING COMPANIES, GOVERNMENTS, EDUCATIONAL GROUPS, AND NGOS

Child labor is a very complex issue which needs to be addressed by a wide range of parties, including companies, governments, educational groups, and NGOs. If companies take unilateral action and simply fire working children, these children may be forced into even more dire circumstances, such as child prostitution or mining. Companies need to work in partnership with other sectors to develop better options for working children. By working with interested parties, companies can find allies and assistance for dealing with the complex issue of child labor through remediation and education.

Compliance with the SA8000 child labor requirements

What can companies do to comply with SA8000's child labor requirements? There are four steps companies need to take to address the child labor issue.

Step 1 Ascertain whether there is a problem

Detection of child labor is often problematic for several reasons:

- documents such as birth certificates or school papers may be falsified or may not exist;
- children may accompany parents to the workplace, but not work themselves;
- children in developing countries may look younger than their counterparts in the North.

Consultations with local NGOs can be helpful in establishing if child labor is a problem in a factory. Local offices of the ILO, UNICEF, development agencies, or schools may also be able to alert companies to problems. (See Appendix for Resources.)

Step 2 Provide immediate protection for children working at the site

"The need to protect under-aged children from exploitative conditions must be balanced with the risk of taking precipitous action(s) that could harm the children or significantly worsen their overall welfare. Children under 13 should be taken out of work and immediately enrolled in a remediation program. They should not simply be dismissed."[3]

"If youth under 18 are working, even if it is part-time/light work, the company should make sure that they are kept away from dangerous equipment and that the conditions of work will not endanger their health."[4]

Step 3 Develop a remediation plan: shifting under-age workers out of the workplace, setting up procedures and guidelines to halt new hires

Even if there are no children working in the site, a company seeking certification must develop a remediation plan, which can be implemented should the need ever arise. (See Chapter 4 for an example.) In addition, companies must develop effective procedures for halting new hires of under-age workers. This can involve training personnel managers to identify under-age workers and/or developing joint programs with local groups or schools who can provide assistance.

Step 4 Find long-term alternatives to the use of under-age workers

"Companies can help prepare adults to take jobs in the industry through training programs. At the same time, they can support/collaborate with local governments or NGOs in creating schools. In most cases, supporting improvements to the state educational system should be prioritized."[5]

⚭ links to other issues addressed in SA8000

Child labor is closely connected to other aspects of SA8000. Often, the existence of children working at a site or in the neighboring areas is a sign that wages are not meeting basic human needs. There is also an important link between child labor, over-time, and homeworking.[6] If working parents are unable to complete their quota, they may take work home, which may be completed by their children. While homeworking is not yet addressed in SA8000, subsequent editions of the standard will address it.

▨ Forced labor

SA8000 definition

Forced labor: All work or service that is extracted from any person under the menace of any penalty for which said person has not offered him/herself voluntarily.

SA8000 provision

SA8000 2.1 *The company shall not engage in or support the use of forced labor, nor shall personnel be required to lodge "deposits" or identity papers upon commencing employment with the company.*

SA8000 prohibits the use of forced or compulsory labor, including bonded, forced, and compulsory prison labor.[7] Bonded labor occurs when a person works to pay off a debt. Prison labor refers here to the use of prisoners who are not paid or who are required to work in order to complete their sentence. Indentured laborers are unable to leave their job without the permission of the employer.[8] While it may be unlikely that a company seeking certification engages in these practices, such abuses may exist further down the supply chain. In some countries, including China, it is common for companies to hire workers through employment agencies which may withhold identity papers. In such cases, the placement agency is considered a supplier.

One of the mechanisms used to coerce workers into working against their will is to require employees to surrender their passport or other key documents to the employer. In this way, workers are unable to leave without access to identity papers. Likewise, workers might be forced to lodge a deposit with the employer. If the employee leaves, he or she must surrender the deposit, making it unlikely that the employee will leave. In some regions, debt bondage is also a problem, with employees forced to purchase goods at a company store or to rent accommodation from the company at very high prices, which they can pay for only by working.

In some instances, the use of training programs is a ruse to avoid paying workers. While the majority of training programs are worthwhile, such programs should not allow a worker to be "trained" – and hence not paid – indefinitely. Job training programs must be temporary in nature.

While forced labor is associated with some developing countries, such practices occur in the USA and Europe, where migrant workers, from countries like China and Thailand, work illegally in sweatshop conditions. Because of their illegal status, these migrants have no recourse to legal remedies.

∞ links to other aspects of SA8000

The presence of forced labor is a likely indication that there are abuses in other areas, such as compensation, disciplinary practices, and working hours. In some parts of South Asia, child bonded labor is a serious issue, which will be discussed in Chapter 6 on Regional concerns.

▥ Health and safety

SA8000 provisions

SA8000 3.1 *The company, bearing in mind the prevailing knowledge of the industry and of any specific hazards, shall provide a safe and healthy working environment and shall take adequate steps to prevent accidents and injury to health arising out of, associated with or occurring in the course of work, by minimizing, so far as is reasonably predictable, the causes of hazards inherent in the working environment;*

SA8000 3.2 *The company shall appoint a senior management representative responsible for the health and safety of all personnel, and accountable for the implementation of the Health and Safety elements of this standard;*

SA8000 3.3 *The company shall ensure that all personnel receive regular and recorded health and safety training, and that such training is repeated for new and reassigned personnel;*

SA8000 3.4 *The company shall establish systems to detect, avoid, or respond to potential threats to the health and safety of all personnel;*

SA8000 3.5 *The company shall provide, for use by all personnel, clean bathrooms, access to potable water, and, if appropriate, sanitary facilities for food storage;*

SA8000 3.6 *The company shall ensure that, if provided for personnel, dormitory facilities are clean, safe, and meet the basic needs of the personnel.*

Most companies seeking to implement SA8000 will have to make improvements in the area of health and safety. This section of SA8000 is very broad and sector-specific. Developing and improving management systems will facilitate improvements to health and safety in the workplace.

While some health and safety improvements can be implemented quickly and with little or no cost, others may require significant change and expense. An example of some of the easier health and safety improvements is clearing fire exits and placing small guards on sewing machines to prevent eye injury. Reviewing health and safety issues may raise complex issues which may require re-engineering

REVIEWING HEALTH AND SAFETY ISSUES MAY RAISE COMPLEX ISSUES WHICH MAY REQUIRE RE-ENGINEERING THE WORK PROCESS TO FIND CREATIVE SOLUTIONS the work process to find creative solutions. For example, in producing shoes, the glues used to connect the mid-sole to the outer-sole can create terrible fumes. Rather than focus on protecting workers through issuing masks, companies are experimenting with water-based chemicals to substitute toxic chemicals.[9] Finding creative solutions requires time and consultation with other companies.

There are three fundamental components to meeting SA8000's requirements in health and safety.

- Management must be held responsible for enforcing preventive measures and enabling compliance by providing adequate resources.
- Workers must be given a voice in the process.
- The focus should be on preventing future problems.

⬤ links to other aspects of SA8000

There are particular health and safety issues linked to young workers. For example, a young worker may not be able to reach a safety switch or safety gear may not fit appropriately. These issues need to be considered carefully.

There may also be links to problems of discrimination, with workers from a minority or disadvantaged group being given more dangerous tasks.

Health and safety issues are also linked to working hours – as workers become over-tired, accidents may become more likely.

Freedom of association and the right to collective bargaining

SA8000 provisions

SA8000 4.1 *The company shall respect the right of all personnel to form and join trade unions of their choice and to bargain collectively;*

SA8000 4.2 *The company shall, in those situations in which the right to freedom of association and collective bargaining are restricted under law, facilitate parallel means of independent and free association and bargaining for all such personnel;*

SA8000 4.3 *The company shall ensure that representatives of such personnel are not the subject of discrimination and that such representatives have access to their members in the workplace.*

It is important to emphasize that SA8000 should not replace the workers' right to unionize or to bargain collectively. Hence in "facilitating parallel means" in restrictive locations, the company can develop workers' committees that focus on the following types of issues:

- health and safety
- productivity and quality
- complaints and resolutions
- social accountability education
- wage negotiations
- community development
- literacy
- benefits.[10]

In cases where a company is required to "facilitate parallel means" of organizing, committees should maintain records of meetings, including dates, number of attendees, and decisions reached. In cases where elections are held, results should be recorded. There should be evidence of a dialogue between the committees and management. The workers should understand how the committees operate, management needs to respond to recommendations developed by the workers' committees.

The Interfaith Center on Corporate Responsibility (ICCR) has issued several recommendations to factories operating in Indonesia where workers' rights are not respected. These recommendations can be useful in other countries where these rights are repressed. ICCR recommends that companies pledge:

a) *to not dismiss workers for attempting to organize an independent union* (as does SA8000);

b) *to not call in the military in the event of a strike; and*

c) *to work with other foreign companies* (whose investments and job creation in Indonesia give them influence) *to oppose the Indonesian government's labor regulations … that would erode the right to form a union and bargain collectively.*[11]

∞ links to other aspects of SA8000

In countries where freedom of association and the right to bargain collectively are restricted by law, wages will most likely be a problem area, as will other elements of SA8000, from health and safety to working hours.

Discrimination

SA8000 provisions

SA8000 5.1   *The company shall not engage in or support discrimination in hiring, compensation, access to training, promotion, termination or retirement based on race, caste national origin, religion, disability, gender, sexual orientation, union membership, or political affiliation.*

SA8000 5.2   *The company shall not interfere with the exercise of the rights of personnel to observe tenets or practices, or to meet needs relating to race, caste, national origin, religion, disability, gender, sexual orientation, union membership, or political affiliation.*

SA8000 5.3   *The company shall not allow behavior, including gestures, language and physical contact, that is sexually coercive, threatening, abusive, or exploitative.*

Discrimination can be based on a range of factors, including gender, age, place of origin, and religion.

Gender-based discrimination

In many societies and sectors, women receive lower pay than their male counterparts for equal work. In many industries, certain lines of work are open only to men, making it difficult for women to advance. There are other types of discrimination against women, including discriminating against pregnant women in hiring, or requiring employees to practice contraception in order to be hired. Both of these issues are addressed in the section on regional concerns (Chapter 6). Sexual harassment is also a form of gender-based discrimination.

Sexual harassment

"involves unwanted behavior of a sexual nature, and a perception by the victim that it has become a condition of work, or creates a hostile, intimidating, and

humiliating working environment. It can involve physical contact, expression of sexual innuendoes, sexually colored comments and jokes, the exhibition of pornography, or unnecessary and unwanted comments on a person's appearance."[12]

Sexual harassment often goes unreported, as its victims feels embarrassed and afraid that their complaints will not be taken seriously or believed.

Discrimination against migrants

With globalization, migration is increasing, leading to greater numbers of migrants in the workplace. According to the ILO, the number of migrant workers is between 36 million and 42 million.[13] These groups are often in a more vulnerable situation than locals, as they are less likely to be fluent in the local language. In some cases, they may be further marginalized by lacking the legal status to work, giving little recourse should abuses take place.

Discrimination is difficult to address as it is often informal in nature. For example, workers from a disadvantaged group may be given older machines, making them more likely to fall short of their production quota. In addition, discrimination may be based in deep-rooted cultural attitudes which make change difficult.

It is not the intention of SA8000 to discount local cultural practice. However, if cultural or religious norms cause certain groups to be disadvantaged in the workplace, then systems may need to be developed to address these issues. In certain societies, men and women are not allowed to work in close proximity. This need not be discriminatory, if both men and women receive equal pay for equal work, under equal conditions, while working in different locations.

The informal nature of discrimination, and its deep roots in cultural bias, highlight the need for effective management systems for preventing abuses. There are several types of management systems which are useful to prevent discrimination.

Training

Discrimination can spring from ignorance, leading to attitudes which foster problems, hence, training those managers involved in making hiring and firing decisions is important. Training is also an effective mechanism for combating sexual harassment. Unions can play an active role in providing training.

Records

Given the informal nature of many forms of discrimination, records provide a degree of formality. Wage slips, job announcements, files of rejected applicants for jobs, and records on the number of people trained can provide a manager with clues as to whether discrimination is a problem within the facility.

Complaints and appeals

An effective complaints and appeals system can provide a recourse for employees who think they have been the victims of discrimination. However, it is important to note that given the sensitive nature of some types of discrimination, such as sexual harassment, that the absence of appeals does not indicate that the workplace is free of discrimination. Workers may simply be too afraid to complain.

Disciplinary practices

SA8000 provisions

SA8000 6.1 *The company shall not engage in or support the use of corporal punishment, mental or physical coercion, and verbal abuse.*

In assessing disciplinary practices, Dominique Gangneux of BVQI looks for a continuum of disciplinary procedures. There should be a gradual process of disciplinary procedures, with a verbal warning, followed by a written warning and possibly some sort of mediation.[14] Company management needs to establish transparent disciplinary rules. Management needs to introduce the workers to the rules during the recruitment stage and on the job. In cases where a verbal warning is issued, it is necessary to understand the root cause of the problem and to provide more training at that time on disciplinary rules. Depending on the gravity of the problem, it may be necessary to have mediation, either by trade union representatives or the SA employee representative or others. National legislation may provide some guidance in this area.[15] The use of fines as a form of punishment is not recommended.

Workers must be aware of rules and participate in the development of policies. Workers need to have access to an appeals process to protect their rights. The complaints and appeals process must be documented and workers should not be fearful of filing an appeal. As with other elements of the standard, companies should maintain records on workers who violate policies.

The Interfaith Center on Corporate Responsibility recommends substituting fines with a bonus system that rewards positive actions. Bonuses can be creative – employers can provide positive incentives such as small gifts or appliances to workers who have suggestions for improvements to health and safety in the workplace.

◐ links to other aspects of SA8000

There may be a link between strict disciplinary practices and forced labor, with such practices used to intimidate and coerce workers from reporting abuses.

▥ Working hours

SA8000 provisions

SA8000 7.1   *The company shall comply with applicable laws and industry standards on working hours, in any event, personnel shall not on a regular basis, be required to work in excess of 48 hours per week and shall be provided with at least one day off for every seven day period.*

SA8000 7.2   *The company shall ensure that over-time work (more than 48 hours per week) does not exceed 12 hours per employee per week, is not demanded other than in exceptional and short-term business circumstances, and is always remunerated at a premium rate.*

Over-time must be voluntary. SAI defines "exceptional business circumstances" as a temporary period of high volume or labor-intensive activity due to emergency conditions and/or conditions that could not have been foreseen. Such periods can include delays caused by natural disaster or violence and problems with delivery of raw materials, but cannot include seasonal or recurring circumstances, such as a holiday rush.[16]

Auditors and companies are reporting some unintended conse-quences of restrictions on working hours. According to Mark Miller, formerly of SGS (now with KPMG), workers often try to circumvent this requirement of SA8000 by seeking extra hours in other factories, which may actually make their work schedules more onerous if the second factory is located at some distance from the first. There are countries where employees voluntarily want to work longer than allowed in the standard, such as the Philippines and Thailand.[17] In China, workers from the provinces leave home and migrate to the cities for a short time, where they hope to earn as much as possible to support their families upon their return. Hence, they wish to work as many hours as possible, so they may return home earlier, despite the fact that Chinese law is often more restrictive than SA8000.

Restricting work hours may also increase the incidence of homeworking. Companies should not rely on homeworking to compensate for fewer working hours. As noted earlier, while SA8000 does not currently address the issue of homeworking, it is expected that subsequent reviews of SA8000 will discuss it.

As in other elements of SA8000, company managers must be aware of local and national norms for working hours, holidays, and breaks.

⊙ links to other issues

The existence of regular over-time may indicate that compensation fails to meet basic human needs, an issue which is addressed in the next section of this book.

Compensation

"A living wage must be determined locally, not in Washington D.C., New York City or Geneva."

Neil Kearney, General Secretary, International Textile, Garment and Leather Workers' Federation[18]

SA8000 provisions

SA8000 8.1 *The company shall ensure that wages paid for a standard working week shall meet at least legal or industry minimum standards and shall always be* *sufficient to meet basic needs of personnel and to provide some discretionary income.*

SA8000 8.2 *The company shall ensure that deductions from wages are not made for disciplinary purposes, and shall ensure that wage and benefits composition are detailed clearly and regularly for workers; the company shall also ensure that wages and benefits are rendered in full compliance with all applicable laws and that compensation is rendered either in cash or check form, in a manner convenient to workers.*

"A manner convenient to workers" is defined by SAI as one that

"ensures workers are not obliged to travel any significant distance or make an extra trip or incur any cost to collect their pay."[19]

SA8000 8.3 *The company shall ensure that labor-only contracting arrangements and false apprenticeship schemes are not undertaken in an effort to avoid fulfilling its obligations to personnel under applicable laws pertaining to labor and social security legislation and regulations.*

A living wage should provide adequately for workers to feed, clothe, and house themselves. According to the *SA8000 Guidance Document*, there are several mechanisms for assessing whether the salary paid meets basic needs.[20] The best approach is to rely on agreements negotiated by trade unions. In the absence of negotiated agreements or trade unions, a company can hire a reputable, independent research organization to assist with this calculation. **In determining a living wage, it is important to balance carefully worker consultations with quantitative methods.**

The basic needs formula

Step 1

Determine the cost of the basic food basket needed for an adequate diet. In the majority of countries this is determined by the local government through national home surveys.

Step 2

Determine what percentage of household income is spent on food. Dividing this percentage into 1 will give a multiplier which, when applied to the cost of the food basket, gives an estimate of what the average household needs to spend per person. This figure is represented by "y" is the sample calculation below.

Step 3

Determine the appropriate number of household members; SAI recommends using half of the average household size for the country or region. This assumes there is at least one other income contributing to the household economy. In a local economy where there is a strong tendency toward single parent households, auditors may need to consider raising this number above half.

Step 4

Determine the percentage multiplier to "provide for some discretionary income." SAI recommends providing at least 10 percent and therefore using a multiplier of at least 110 percent.

Step 5

Insert the defined numbers into the following formula:

[Basic food basket × (1/y% of average household income spent on food) × (0.5 × average household size) × 110%].

Example: Assuming the basic food basket costs $15 per week, the average household size in the country is 5.6 people, and the percentage of income spent on food is 40 percent, then the estimated basic needs wage would be $115.50 per week calculated as follows:

$15.00 (1/40%) × (0.5 × 5.6) × 110% = $115.50.

Step 6

Analyze the quality of the data and verify results using a local consultant. Remember that the government-determined basic food basket may be inflated or deflated for political reasons, hence it should only be used as a comparison, not as a precise guide.

Company managers can consult with auditors to assess if the food basket meets the minimum international standard of a daily diet of 2100 calories; that prices assigned to the foodstuffs adequately reflect the current market situation; and that subsidies and severe inflation have been taken into account where necessary.[21]

Assessing a living wage is not a simple task for several reasons: first, family size varies. In some regions and sectors, the minimum wage or the prevailing wage may not meet basic needs. The number of children also varies significantly in different regions and within regions. It is important to emphasize that time is allocated for companies to come into compliance with this section of SA8000. At certification, the company needs only to calculate the basic needs wage, pay the minimum wage, and set up a plan to get to a living wage with a timetable. Progress against the timetable will be monitored by the auditor.

Companies should not expect the auditor or certification body to set a living wage. The auditor is simply assessing that there is a system in place to ensure that workers receive a living wage. There are several reasons why this is the case: first, if certification bodies were to set the living wage, there would be pressure among certification bodies to compete on the basis of who approves the lowest living wage. Second, the auditor is only present every six months, so that if a major devaluation or economic crisis were to occur in the interim between audits, there needs to be a mechanism in place to ensure that workers are still receiving a living wage.[22] It is important to emphasize that more research needs to be done in this area. Fortunately, a number of institutions are carrying out work in this area.

Chapter 4 is the "nuts and bolts" chapter of this book, providing all the necessary information on implementing the management systems of SA8000. The chapter begins by defining management systems and then continues with a section on how to get started by using the plan-do-check-act model. As in Chapter 3, be sure to refer to the *Guidance Document* for SA8000. The chapter contains best practices culled from existing companies. In some cases, these sample forms have been improved by experts as the book was edited. There is a significant gap between what is mandated by SA8000 (in the code) and what is best practice, hence not all of the items in the checklists provided are mandatory. SAI plans to include the forms in this chapter and others on the SAI website so they can be easily downloaded and completed and sent to suppliers.

4

An implementation guide on developing management systems

The management systems of SA8000 are of fundamental importance, differentiating SA8000 from principles, statements of intent, and most codes of conduct. SA8000's requirements for management systems ensure that social issues are integrated into all aspects of company policy and ensure its day-to-day operations. It is the management systems that guarantee that social policies are in effect long after an auditor leaves and that provide documentation for auditors. The management systems of SA8000 also assure that there will be continuous improvement in the social conditions of the workplace.

Management systems include: training programs, communications, elected representatives, management representatives with adequate budgets, clear lines of authority, management reviews, control of suppliers, and planning, as well as policies, procedures, forms, and checklists for recording compliance with each portion of the standard. By integrating SA8000 into these systems, SA8000 becomes part of the culture of the company. This chapter seeks to assist companies to implement and improve their management systems in order to successfully adopt SA8000.

Devising management systems for SA8000 can seem like a daunting task. Once devised, however, management systems tend to pay off in a significant manner. This chapter contains practical advice, excerpts from the SA8000 Guidance Document, as well as sample policies used by leading companies. This book and supplementary materials on the SA8000 website (www.SA-intl.org) are designed to help you set up your company's management systems.

There are many tools available to companies seeking help in developing management systems for SA8000. SA8000 training courses, offered around the world, provide many resources and contacts for managers as well as auditors. The SA8000 Guidance Document is also an excellent resource for companies. Both the training sessions and the Guidance Document are designed for training both auditors and managers seeking certification. Companies benefit by absorbing the background and language of the auditor. Contacts for these resources are available at the end of the book and on the SAI website.

According to Mark Miller, former Corporate Business Manager for the Global Program for Social Accountability at SGS (now at KPMG),

"A management gap exists. Management systems are difficult to implement, unless the company has a pre-existing management system. If there is no preexisting management system, then it can be challenging to implement SA8000. The reality is that it is hard for medium-sized companies to develop management systems."[1]

This chapter contains the necessary tools for creating and improving the management systems necessary for SA8000.

The Plan-Do-Check-Act model

In order to facilitate implementation, it is useful to divide the process into four parts, using the Plan-Do-Check-Act model.

Plan

During the planning stage, carefully review the SA8000 standard and conduct a self-assessment of your company. The self-assessment will reveal the shape and magnitude of the task ahead; it will indicate strengths and weaknesses. Nearly all companies will need to make improvements and many of these will prove highly beneficial to your company's bottom line. The key to planning is prioritizing which problem areas should be addressed first. Urgency should be given to areas where worker safety is at risk. At this time, it is useful to develop a list of the interested parties with whom the company will seek partnerships to ensure successful implementation of SA8000. One self-assessment tool available to managers is the CD ROM developed by Compusense known as ComPass (see Resources in Appendix for details).

In the planning phase, it is useful to consider strategic issues as well. Is the facility or company already certified to other standards, such as ISO9000 or ISO14000, or is the company planning such certifications? Having management systems for other standards tends to facilitate implementation. If the facility has developed management systems for ISO9000 and ISO14000, it may make sense to integrate management systems and audits, rather than developing parallel systems. Integrated audits are discussed in Chapter 8.

Do

Inform workers about SA8000 and allow space and time for workers to elect their own SA8000 representatives (the SA8000 representative is discussed in detail on page 66 of this chapter). If the facility is unionized, the trade union representative should be asked to organize the election so as not to create a parallel work organization that could cause friction later on. Using the models of best practice in this book, develop policies on social issues with the involvement of workers. Create an internal SA8000 Manual, which incorporates the standard, and the company's policies. Develop training programs, using the SA8000 Manual to raise awareness among workers. Begin consultations with interested parties. Implement the clauses of SA8000, giving special priority to the safety of workers. At this time, all suppliers should be notified about SA8000.

Check

A full audit should be scheduled once internal monitoring indicates that the company is "audit ready," i.e. close to or fully meeting the standard. A pre-audit can be a useful tool for determining whether a facility is ready for a full audit. The pre-audit is less expensive and less time-consuming, and can save resources if the facility is unsure that it is audit ready. Accredited certification firms can perform pre-audits. Consulting firms can be helpful in developing or improving management systems and getting the facility audit ready. It is important to emphasize that there are conflicts of interest guidelines which preclude accredited certification bodies from consulting.

To check the qualifications of a consultant, be sure he or she has successfully completed an accredited SA8000 course and check references

with other clients. Ask to see a certificate of course completion or check with SAI for listings of trained consultants. Be sure to check that the consultant is fluent in the language spoken by employees and that they are familiar with local law and with NGOs in the area. Most companies will need to take corrective actions based on the audit. As of Fall 2000, all SA8000-certified companies received Corrective Action Requests (CARS) and implemented corrective actions to qualify.

Act

SA8000 is a system of continuous improvement, which incorporates feedback from multiple sources: employees, interested parties, auditors, etc. SA8000 requires companies to conduct regular management reviews to prevent problems from occurring. Hence, companies continue to implement SA8000 once they have received certification.

This chapter is based on best practices of companies currently implementing SA8000 and provides guidance on the following issues:

- developing a social accountability policy
- appointing SA8000 representatives
- planning and implementing your SA8000 management system
- controlling suppliers
- conducting risk analysis
- addressing concerns and taking corrective action
- training
- maintaining records
  - checklist of documents
  - child labor policy
  - apprenticeship program
  - forced labor policy
  - health and safety policy

- policy on freedom of association and the right to collective bargaining
- anti-discrimination policy
- policy on disciplinary practices
- policy on working hours
- compensation policy
- policy on management systems.

The following section of this chapter contains SA8000's requirements for management systems with sample policies and forms developed by companies currently implementing the standard. The sample policies and forms can be adopted for use in a company's manual. These forms and other material can also be downloaded from the SAI website to facilitate implementation.

Developing a social accountability policy

Although management systems is the last provision listed in SA8000, it is the one that corporate managers should start with.

SA8000 provision

SA8000 9.1 *Top management shall define the company's policy for social accountability and labor conditions to ensure that it:*

a) *includes a commitment to conform to all requirements of this standard and requirements to which the company subscribes;*

b) *includes a commitment to comply with national and other applicable law, and to respect the international instruments listed in Section II and their interpretation;[2]*

c) *includes a commitment to continual improvement;*

d) *is effectively documented, implemented, maintained, communicated and is accessible in a comprehensible form to all personnel, including, directors, executives, management supervisors, and staff, whether directly employed, contracted or otherwise representing the company;*

e) *is publicly available.*

The social accountability policy (SAP) should define the measures put in place to ensure ongoing compliance with SA8000. This policy should cover every element in the standard. Upon being hired, every worker should receive a copy of the SAP in a language they are fluent in. Within a set period of time of being hired, such as one month, new staff should be introduced to the SAP through training.[3]

Figure 4.1 ■ Sample social accountability policy

Company X is committed to producing high quality products in a manner that demonstrates sound business ethics, adherence to local and national laws and an absolute regard for human rights. Company X requires the same standards from our suppliers and will not knowingly enter into business relationships with any company that does not share these core values.

Child labor
Hire only workers who meet or exceed minimum legal age requirements or, if workers are found to be under age, then provide means for remediation and education.

Forced labor
Prohibit the use of prison, convict, forced, or indentured labor.

Health and safety
Provide a safe and healthy working environment, with a focus on training, awareness, and accident prevention.

Freedom of association and collective bargaining
Respect the right of employees to join trade unions and to bargain collectively or, if such rights are restricted under law, to facilitate parallel means of free association.

Discrimination
Promote an atmosphere free of discrimination.

Disciplinary practices
Prohibit corporal punishment, abuse, or harassment.

Working hours
Comply with applicable laws and industry standards on working hours, not to exceed 48 hours per week on a regular basis, plus a maximum of 12 hours per week of over-time (paid at a premium), with at least one day off each week.

Compensation
Offer compensation that meets local minimum wage standards and provides for basic needs and discretionary income.

Management systems
Implement a management system that ensures compliance and continued improvement of the company's performance against our code of conduct.

Some companies may wish to implement a SAP which also addresses environmental or other issues not addressed in SA8000. For example, companies may want to review SAI's feasibility study on integrity and anti-corruption measures. The Global Reporting Initiative (GRI) is developing guidelines for environmental reporting. The Forestry Stewardship Council has standards and accredits certifiers for sustainably-harvested wood. The Marine Stewardship Council provides important certifications for companies in the fishing industry, and IFOAM provides certifications for organic produce.

Some companies report that the process of meeting to discuss a SAP helps to engender the necessary commitment and support for it from within the organization.

Appointing and electing SA8000 representatives

SA8000 provision

SA8000 9.3 *The company shall appoint a senior management representative who, irrespective of other responsibilities, shall ensure that the requirements of this standard are met.*

The social accountability management representative can be either an individual or a committee. The representative(s) must be qualified, e.g. trained in health and safety issues and senior enough within the company to have the requisite authority as well as an adequate budget. SAI recommends that the SA8000 management representative attend an SA8000 training course.

Figure 4.2 ■ Senior management representative, sample job description

– ensure that the organization meets the requirements of SA8000.
– ensure that there is a confidential and accessible system for employees to file complaints related to social issues.
– ensure that adequate funds are allocated for improvements.
– provide incentives for staff to comply with SA8000.

SA8000 provision

SA8000 9.4   *The company shall provide for non-management personnel to choose a representative from their own group to facilitate communication with senior management on matters related to this standard.*

Elections should take place on a regular basis, for example, yearly. One possible mechanism is to request that two or three employees put their names forward. Where unions exist, they should decide the election process. Under no circumstance should the SA8000 representative replace the union.

Figure 4.3 ■ SA8000 representative, sample job description

The SA8000 representative shall:

- participate in monitoring and audit meetings

- hold meetings with workers at regularly scheduled intervals

- assure that minutes are taken at these meetings and maintain them in a logbook

- train workers in SA8000 system

- encourage workers to support and comply with regulations as well as identify potential hazards

- convey complaints to managers

- when complaints are made, track progress and inform workers on the resolution.

Appointing a senior manager

SA8000 (3.2) requires the company to assign responsibility for health and safety to a senior management representative. Accountability must be documented from senior management to line supervisors. Resources, such as time and funding, must be projected and granted to the staff charged with specific tasks and objectives.

Figure 4.4 is an example of a job description for a senior management representative, health and safety, which has been taken from a US company.

Figure 4.4 ■ Health and safety senior management representative, sample job description

Job title: Health and safety senior management representative

Position description
Responsible for the health and safety of all personnel; accountable for the implementation of the health and safety elements of the company policy.

Requirements
Understanding of, and commitment to, the company's health and safety policy.

SA8000 training as well as training in H&S issues such as fire prevention and dealing with toxic chemicals and any other potential hazards iin the workplace.

Responsibilities:

1. Oversee the implementation of the company's health and safety policy.

2. Maintain open communication with non-management health and safety representative on issues of concern to employees.

3. Ensure that H&S training for personnel is effective.

4. Establish and maintain comprehensive systems to detect, avoid, or respond to potential threats to the H&S of all personnel.

5. Provide signs in all worker languages describing emergency procedures and evacuation plan.

6. Ensure that workplace conditions, including work areas, lavatories, food storage facilities and, dormitories, are clean and safe.

7. Provide guidelines for the use of protective gear.

8. Provide guidelines for the storage of hazardous substances.

9. Maintain rotation schedules regulating the amount of time workers are exposed to extremes in temperatures and toxins.

10. Oversee regular inspections of the workplace to ensure compliance with policy and local law and to meet the H&S needs of employees.

11. Establish procedures for remedial action for preventable accidents of hazardous conditions.

12. Oversee inspections of fire extinguishers, sprinklers, air quality, water quality, etc.; take remedial action as required following inspections.

In addition to these requirements stipulated on page 67 by a US clothing company, SAI also recommends the following additional requirements for the senior management health and safety representative.

Figure 4.5 ■ SAI recommended additional requirements for senior management health and safety representative

13. Oversee regular tests on air quality in cases where the site may produce hazardous fumes or particulate pollution and tests on water to ensure that water is potable.

14. Ensure that fire drills take place at least once per year.

15. Periodically review national and local regulations to ensure that the facility is in full compliance with amendments and new regulations.

16. Review accident reports to assess patterns and determine preventive measures.

17. Ensure that workers have a voice in developing procedures and interpreting patterns of accidents.

18. Respond to all H&S concerns and complaints.

19. Report to a senior person within the company, for example, the SA8000 management representative or environmental director.

A non-management health and safety representative is not required under SA8000, but some companies have found that having such a representative helps to disseminate and build support for H&S measures among workers.

Figure 4.6 ■ Job description for a non-management health and safety representative

Job title: Non-management health and safety representative

Position description
Responsible for implementing the company's health and safety policy and communicating staff needs to management.

Requirements
Understanding of, and commitment to, the company's health and safety policy.
Willingness/ability to carry out the elements of this policy in a timely and organized manner.
Ability to communicate well with management.

Responsibilities

1. Maintain open communication with management H&S representative on issues of concern to the employees.

2. Train new and existing personnel in H&S, maintain schedule and attendance checklist.

3. Maintain fire drill log.

4. Arrange for periodic training/re-training of selected personnel in first aid and CPR procedures.

5. Enforce the use of protective gear; maintain checklist for observation and use of protective gear.

6. Maintain checklist for sanitation, cleaning of bathrooms and eating areas.

7. Maintain checklist for safe food storage, including refrigeration control.

8. Maintain accident report forms.

9. Oversee regular inspections of workplace to ensure compliance with policy and local law and to meet the H&S needs of employees.

10. Regularly observe workplace conditions and report findings to management H&S representative.

11. Schedule regular inspections of fire extinguishers, sprinklers, air quality, water quality, etc.; report findings to management.

12. Maintain first aid kit in working order.

It is good practice to share audit reports and reports filed by labor inspectors with SA8000 representatives within the company.

Planning and implementing your SA8000 management system

SA8000 provisions

SA8000 9.2 *Top management shall periodically review the adequacy, suitability, and continuing effectiveness of the company's policy, procedures, and performance results vis à vis the requirements of this standard and other requirements to which the company subscribes. System amendments and improvements shall be implemented where appropriate.*

SA8000 9.5   *The company shall ensure that the requirements of this standard are understood and implemented at all levels of the organization; methods shall include, but are not limited to:*

a) *clear definition of roles, responsibilities, and authority;*

b) *training of new and/or temporary employees upon hiring;*

c) *periodic training and awareness programs for existing employees;*

d) *continuous monitoring of activities and results to demonstrate the effectiveness of systems implemented to meet the company's policy and the requirements of this standard.*

Successful implementation of SA8000 management systems requires clear job descriptions, lines of authority, and corresponding budgets. While there are key people who are responsible for SA8000, all employees must play an active role in its implementation. However, only with adequate training can all employees be empowered to work on implementation. There are several things managers can do to send a message about the vital role of SA8000 within the organization. While not required under SA8000, it is advisable to make the implementation of SA8000 an important part of the criteria for raises and promotion of managers. Emphasis on training and awareness also sends positive messages.

SUCCESSFUL IMPLEMENTATION OF SA8000 MANAGEMENT SYSTEMS REQUIRES CLEAR JOB DESCRIPTIONS, LINES OF AUTHORITY, AND CORRESPONDING BUDGETS

The SA8000 manual plays a critical role in implementing the management systems of the standard. The manual should define roles, responsibilities, and authority for management systems. An important component of the training of all employees, the manual should be accessible at all times to workers. Employees must be aware of the location of the manual.

Continuous monitoring of results is very significant, as it allows for a feedback loop. By gauging the benefits of implementation, employees will feel more empowered to implement the management systems. Such feedback can also be helpful in convincing recalcitrant suppliers about the business benefits of implementing SA8000.

Controlling suppliers

SA8000 provisions

SA8000 9.6 *The company shall establish and maintain appropriate procedures to evaluate and select suppliers based on their ability to meet the requirements of this standard.*

SA8000 9.7 *The company shall maintain appropriate records of suppliers' commitment to social accountability, including, but not limited to, the suppliers' written commitment to:*

a) conform to all requirements of this standard (including this clause)

b) participate in the company's monitoring activities as requested;

c) promptly remediate any non conformance identified against the requirements of this standard;

d) promptly and completely inform the company of any and all relevant business relationship(s) with other supplier(s) and subcontractor(s).

SA8000 9.8 *The company shall maintain reasonable evidence that the requirements of this standard are being met by suppliers and subcontractors.*

Control of suppliers is one of the most complex and essential aspects of SA8000, for several reasons.

- It can be immensely difficult for a small company to require major changes of a large company.

- If a company has many suppliers, located at great distance, it may be difficult to identify companies, establish management systems and visit suppliers and subcontractors.

- Agents are reluctant to release the names and location of suppliers.

As more and more companies require their suppliers to conform to SA8000, control of suppliers will become easier. According to Frits Nagel of WE Europe,

"It will be very helpful when our suppliers are also forced to apply for the certificate by other big buyers. Until now, most of our suppliers tell WE Europe that we are the only buyer asking them to implement SA8000."[4]

In return for implementing SA8000, most suppliers expect a promise for long-term contracts and even preferential treatment.[5] Signatory members of SA8000 meet regularly and can create incentives to attract big suppliers to conform to SA8000.

How can a company monitor its suppliers and subcontractors? SA8000 gives companies flexibility in deciding how best to control their suppliers' adherence to SA8000. WE Europe writes to each supplier and provides the following text.

Figure 4.7 ■ WE Europe supplier questionnaire[6]

We herewith request that you indicate with a cross which of the following statements is applicable in your situation:

Short-term

☐ Yes, our company complies with the national Laws and Regulations relating to working conditions in the areas of age, working hours and health and safety for its workers.

☐ No, our company does not yet comply with the National Laws relating to working conditions because _____

_____

Medium-term

☐ Yes, we comply with the requirements of the "Code of Conduct for WE Europe" as supplied to us.[6]

Long-term

☐ Yes, we fully comply with all the requirements of the SA8000 standard for Social Accountability and will consider when we will be ready to apply for the SA8000 certificate.

☐ In the meantime, we have already contacted SGS, BVQI, DNV, UL, or ITS for further information.

Companies should ask their suppliers to disclose their social objectives, followed by the process of continuous improvement related to these objectives in subsequent years. A basic rule of thumb adopted by SGS is that if suppliers are local, the company should visit them; if they are some distance away, then visits may not be feasible and other forms of communication may be needed. It cannot be emphasized enough that this rule of thumb applies to secondary suppliers, not to signatory members of SA8000.[7] Signatory members need to disclose to the public, on an annual basis, the independently verified information listed in Fig. 4.8.

Figure 4.8 ■ **Information which signatory members must disclose annually**

A. SA8000 applicants

1. The number of its suppliers and its own production facilities that have attained SA8000 Applicant status at the end of the report year (and, as applicable, for the previous year and cumulative).

2. For comparison, the number of SA8000 Applicants set as an objective by the Signatory Member company for the report year.

3. The number of SA8000 Applicants set as an objective by the Signatory Member Company for the forthcoming year(s).

B. SA8000 certified suppliers

1. The number of its suppliers and its own production facilities that are currently certified for compliance with SA8000 at the end of the report year (and, as applicable, for the previous year and cumulative).

2. For comparison, the number of SA8000 certified suppliers and production facilities set as an objective by the Signatory Member company for the report year.

3. The number of SA8000 certified suppliers and facilities set as an objective by the Signatory Member for the forthcoming year(s).

C. Universe of suppliers

The Signatory Member's universe of suppliers, e.g. the approximate number of suppliers each year. The number can be expressed in rounded numbers or as a range.

There is additional material that can be disclosed on an *optional* basis. See Chapter 7 on Communication.

According to Naldo Dantas, of Bahia Sul, a Brazilian company and pulp producer, it is useful for companies to conduct a risk analysis of their suppliers in order to ascertain problems.[8]

Conducting risk analysis

Risk factors which need to be considered include the following.

1. Industry

Health and safety concerns are industry-specific. Certain products may signal high risks to worker health, including those involving toxic glues (in manufacturing shoes), those with high pesticide use, etc. Some products, such as brass, have a higher incidence of child labor than other products.

2. Location

Is the supplier located in a region where there is a high incidence of discrimination, or of forced or child labor?

3. History

Does the supplier have a poor record in worker safety? In freedom of association? Has the supplier changed its name frequently? (This practice could indicate legal problems.) Consultations with trade unions and labor inspectorates can be helpful in signaling and assessing previous problems.

4. Length of supply chain

The longer the supply chain, the harder it becomes to screen for problems. For example, companies with shameful social practices may hide behind other suppliers with good records or behind agents and buying houses which conceal their identities.

5. Company size

In analyzing its supply chain, Otto Versand has observed that the smaller the company, the worse its social performance tends to be. Small companies may have fewer resources than their large counterparts, but greater flexibility in making changes. Management systems also differ based on company size. The larger the company, the more likely it is to have management systems in place. Smaller companies tend to rely on more informal systems.

THE LARGER THE COMPANY, THE MORE LIKELY IT IS TO HAVE MANAGEMENT SYSTEMS IN PLACE.

Risk analysis informs company strategy. Some companies decide to work on SA8000 first with suppliers in the highest risk areas. Other companies seek to replace high-risk suppliers with better suppliers. (Companies are advised by SAI not to dump suppliers with poor records, but to work with them to seek to improve working conditions. The goal of SA8000 is to promote workers' rights globally. Cutting ties with poor suppliers may not curtail abuses, as that supplier may simply continue to produce for other customers.) Some companies start with their largest suppliers, in order to ensure that a significant percentage of their supplier base is socially responsible. Another strategy used by some companies is to begin implementation in certain geographic regions, deemed most important by stakeholders due to high risk, lack of rule of law, or government enforcement.

Addressing concerns and taking corrective action

SA8000 provisions

SA8000 9.9   *The company shall investigate, address, and respond to the concerns of employees and other interested parties with regard to conformance/non-conformance with the company's policy and/or the requirements of this standard; the company shall refrain from disciplining, dismissing or otherwise discriminating against any employee for providing information concerning observance of the standard.*

SA8000 9.10   *The company shall implement remedial and corrective action and allocate adequate resources appropriate to the nature and severity of any non-conformance identified against the company's policy and/or the requirements of the standard.*

Many companies are finding it useful to place suggestion boxes in the workplace, asking workers to list their concerns. Some companies are experimenting with a self-mailer in which employees mail in their comments anonymously to the company. Reebok is piloting a self-mailer among its contractors, asking them to provide one to each employee along with a pay-check. Reebok's code of conduct is printed on the back of the mailer. Whether complaints are made in person or in writing, it is useful and necessary to track these comments in a log, listing the complaint, a proposed remedial course of action, and how and when the issue is addressed. Trade unions can also play a role in receiving complaints, with labor representatives phoning in or emailing problems.

A useful approach to addressing the concerns of workers is to implement an open-door policy. A manager at the Chang Shin Vietnam Co. reports that such a policy allows workers to voice their concerns. Workers avail themselves of the policy on a daily basis to report conflicts with supervisors or even to request improvements to the lunch menu.[9] The elected SA8000 representative needs to let workers know that they can convey complaints to him or her and that the representative will track progress and inform workers on the resolution

Training

Training is a fundamental aspect of SA8000, as it promotes collaboration and buy-in from workers. Training can also serve as a bridge to interested parties. Unions should play an important role in training. SAI and the International Textile, Garment and Leather Workers' Federation (ITGLWF) are developing a training program to increase awareness of SA8000 around the world. Moreover, SA8000 courses are offered around the world, with free places reserved for union and NGO representatives.

The SA8000 Manual, with all of the policies of the company, can serve as a text for training. Each worker should own a copy of the manual or should have ready access to a copy at all times.

The SA8000 *Guidance Document* is also a useful source of information in creating a manual and developing training programs.

Key aspects of training include:

- an introduction to SA8000;
- an introduction to the company's SAP and other policies;
- identification of the SA8000 representatives to whom workers can go with suggestions or problems. Other key issues include how these representatives are elected, the importance of regular meetings, the role of the representative in keeping workers and managers informed;
- health and safety training. The training must emphasize the importance of using protective devices and identify workplace hazards;
- the importance of reporting accidents and preventing their recurrence;
- promoting diversity and eliminating sexual harassment.

Training should be viewed as an ongoing exercise during the career of all employees. In addition to training courses, learning about social issues should be ongoing. One mechanism for increasing worker awareness on a regular basis is to provide reminders of SA8000. SAI has posters of SA8000 and its requirements in several languages. Some companies also provide each worker with a wallet-size card with the key provisions of the code. Other companies are putting key parts of the code on the back of security badges, along with health and safety advice.

Health and safety training

SA8000 (3.3) requires that all personnel receive health and safety training on a regular basis and that this training be recorded. It is important to maintain a log with the name of each employee who participates in the training sessions. While H&S has sector-specific elements, training should address the following issues:

■ Optimal use of safety equipment, such as masks, goggles, etc.
  – when such equipment should be used
  – problems associated with the non-use of equipment
  – how to address problems associated with using safety equipment, such as heat, in the case of use of protective gear to protect from pesticides
■ First aid
  – where the first aid supplies are kept
  – who is trained to use them
  – if locked, who has the key?

Maintaining records

SA8000 provision

SA8000 9.13 *The company shall maintain appropriate records to demonstrate conformance to the requirements of this standard.*

Companies should maintain records on subcontractors, including name, address, type, and quantity of product supplied, and a registry of suppliers' social profiles.

Here is a model checklist based on the one in use by a US company to monitor compliance of suppliers to SA8000. (Note: The sections that are not part of the original document but were added by experts are marked with *.)

Figure 4.9 ■ Checklist of supplier compliance with SA8000

Child labor

■ Child labor company policy

■ Policy on working hours, hazardous equipment, tasks they are not allowed to perform, or other restrictions for young workers

■ Inclusion of policies in employee manual

■ Checklist on application form of appropriate documents for age verification

■ Checklist item in employee personnel file of copy of verification document included in file

■ Schedule of local school hours affecting young workers

■ Location of nearby schools*

■ Basic remediation plan and guidelines for any children found to be working

■ Information on any educational programs offered for young apprentices or interns.*

Note: For those companies where child labor problems are unlikely, this section will be relatively easy.

Forced labor

■ Company policy on forced labor

■ Employment contract if any, including voluntary nature of employment, freedom to leave and procedures to quit. Any statement pertaining to penalties associated with leaving or ceasing work

■ Security positions: job description

■ Security position: sign in and out sheet for employees (The existence of such a sign-in sheet may signal that the workers are not able to come and go freely.)

Health and Safety

■ Health and Safety company policy

■ Company Health and Safety training manual

■ Schedule for employee Health and Safety training

■ A log indicating which employees have or have not completed the training course (Workers should sign that they have completed course.*)

■ Attendance checklist

■ Training specification for those trained in first aid

■ Training specification for training course instructor

■ Senior management representative: job description on issues of H&S (see above)

■ Policy on protective gear

- Checklist for observation and correct use of protective gear
- Policy on level of lighting, air quality, water quality, and frequency of testing
- Reports on level of lighting, air quality, water quality, and water potability tests
- Lists of contents of first aid kit
- Toxic chemicals/hazardous substances: procedures for identifying, labeling, and proper handling
- Procedures and checklist for sanitation, cleaning of toilets, and eating areas
- Procedures and checklist for safe food storage with refrigeration temperature control
- Accident report forms
- Procedure for outside medical emergency assistance
- Format for remedial action for accidents or conditions found to be hazardous
- Procedures and checklist for fire drills, evacuation plan, fire extinguisher, sprinkler maintenance and testing, cleaning and observance of clear aisle and exits.
- Records of visits from inspectors and auditors.

Freedom of association and collective bargaining

- Company policy on collective bargaining
- Policies to include procedures for voting and the use of company facilities or grounds for meetings
- Description of worker committees
- Policy on how, what, and when representatives for workers are elected
- Description of relationship between management representatives and non-management representative
- Meetings: frequency, format for minutes, distribution routing of minutes
- If a union exists, copies of all agreements between the company and the union.

Discrimination

- Company policy on discrimination
- Company policy on sexual harassment
- Company policy on hiring and employment during pregnancy
- Non-discriminatory employment application form
- Guidelines for non-discriminatory employment interviews
- Discrimination complaint form and complaint procedure
- Analysis of pay and promotion by gender
- Schedule of discrimination awareness training sessions and logs of attendees and non-attendees

▶

- Training course outline
- Remediation policies for discrimination violations
- List of qualifications for awareness trainer/job description of awareness trainer
- Copies of advertisements used for soliciting employees (These should not include specifications as to gender, age, or ethnic and religious groups.*)
- Personnel file table of contents checklist.

Disciplinary practices
- Company disciplinary and performance review policy
- Company disciplinary and performance appeals procedure
- Performance review form
- Forms: (1) need for improvement; (2) warning; (3) corrective action form; and (4) appeal form
- List of rules which if violated result in disciplinary action. (Specify the action severity for each infraction.)
- Directions to obtain forms and to whom to appeal
- Description of availability of appeals procedure policy to workers representatives or advocates within or outside the company (unions or NGOs).

Working hours
- Policy on working hours, specifying maximum work week required, days off (vacation and personal), sick days, no homework,[10] break, and lunch
- Maximum over-time and circumstances for which over-time is demanded vs. voluntary and pay rate calculation for over-time
- Piecework program and its relation to over-time
- Unit productivity in comparison to hours worked (and number of employees) form[11]
- Forms detailing units shipped per time period forms.[12]

Compensation
- Compensation policy, including a description of minimum wage requirements, over-time wage, training, apprentice and/or temporary wage
- Documentation of circumstances that could involve deduction of wages, specifying the amount or manner of calculation of each deduction
- Time and method of payment (cash, check or other), timeliness of remuneration
- Evaluation of adequacy of wages to meet basic needs.

Management systems

■ Policy on frequency and depth of top management review of social accountability issues and assignment of senior management representative

■ Policy on method of choosing non-management personnel to represent workers to management

■ Job description of management and non-management representatives for social issues

■ Letters to, forms, purchase orders, and/or contracts with suppliers which delineates suppliers' responsibilities to comply with social standards

■ Policy and description of programs for suppliers, including dealing with compliance and corrective action

■ Policy of public and other access to company's performance on social issues

■ Supplier pre-contract screening forms

■ Checklist for supplier audits (can be the same as this checklist)
  – policy on other language translation of policies
  – identity of SA8000 Manager.*

The Company Manual

The *Company Manual* is a very important document, where the management systems are centralized and introduced to workers. The manual should contain many of the documents listed above and also:

■ company policies, rules, and guidelines

■ child labor policy and restrictions on young workers

■ forced labor policy including voluntary nature of employment

■ health and safety policy including requirements for training, protective gear, job hazards, accident reporting, etc.

■ freedom of association policy including right to organize, use of company facilities, any existing union agreements or contracts, elections

■ disciplinary policy including performance review policy and frequency, rules and consequences of infractions to rules, appeal procedures, and worker representative or advocate rules

- working hour and compensation policies including work week, overtime, days off, vacation, personal or sick days, breaks, meal times, piecework, use of time cards, training or apprenticeship wage, all deductions, time and method of payment
- policy on management commitment to social accountability codes including commitment to standard and law, continuous improvement documentation, public accessibility, frequency of management review, identification of company representatives and their rules, commitment to control of suppliers, records and access to information by interested parties.

While SA8000's management systems require the maintenance of checklists, it is important to emphasize that, while they are helpful, checklists are only a part of the whole. Checklists and other records require training, staff, and budgets to develop a management system.

The next section contains policies and forms currently in use by a major US company, including:

- child labor policy
  - school attendance checklist
- forced labor policy
- health and safety policy
  - accident report form
- policy on freedom of association and the right to collective bargaining
- anti-discrimination policy
- policy on disciplinary practices
- policy on working hours
- compensation policy.

The following forms on child labor are currently in use at a garment facility.

Figure 4.10 ■ Child labor policy form

Child labor policy

The compulsory age for school attendance in this locality is _____

The required (days and) hours of school attendance are _____

The minimum age for work eligibility in this facility by local law is _____

(The Facility) will not tolerate the use of child labor in our facility. Workers must be at least age 15, not younger than the compulsory age to be in school, and be at least the minimum age required by local law for work eligibility in this type of work environment.

If a child worker is found among our employees, a program of remediation will be put in place as follows:

Any child under 13 will be immediately removed from the work-site and placed in a full-time education program. For children age 13 or 14, the remediation program will include education (either returning the child to school OR providing a classroom education on the premises) and, under certain circumstances, part-time light employment, as long as it does not interfere with school hours. Combined time spent at school and work, together with transportation to and from work and school, will not exceed 10 hours per day. To ensure the welfare of the child's family, we may also employ another family member in the child's place.

For all children returning to school, *(The Facility)* will cover the cost of school supplies, clothing, textbooks, and transportation as needed so as not to incur additional expense for the family.

If young workers (age 15–18) are employed in our facility, measures will be taken to protect them from health hazards, such as toxic chemicals, heavy loads, and excessive work hours. Furthermore, young workers will be permitted to work only during daylight hours.

(While not part of this policy, it is advisable that the child labor policy requires that equipment operated by young workers be appropriate for their size.)

Figure 4.11 ■ Apprenticeship program statement

A. *(The Facility)* does not have an apprenticeship program or
B. *(The Facility)* does have an apprenticeship program, which is described as follows:

_____

_____

_____

Figure 4.12 ■ Checklist for recording school attendance

School attendance checklist

Factory name _____

Child's name _____

School name _____

Date	Time-in	Time-out	Teacher signature	Comments

Figure 4.13 ■ Forced labor policy

(The Facility) will not tolerate the use of forced labor, whether in the form of prison labor, indentured labor, bonded labor, or otherwise. Employment at *(the Facility)* is voluntary; under no circumstances will hiring be contingent upon bribes, deposits, or other forms of coercion. No penalties will be incurred in these situations, and employees will be fully paid for all work performed.

Employees are always free to leave at the end of the work-day and to resign from their jobs without any stated cause. Workers are not required to forfeit their identity papers.

(The Facility) will not purchase materials or services from any facility utilizing forced labor as defined above.

Figure 4.14 ■ Health and Safety policy

It is the policy of *(the Facility)* to provide and maintain a safe and healthy work environment for our employees, as well as to make every effort to prevent accidents and injury to health associated with or occurring in the course of work. For this reason, we have established safety rules and regulations to be observed by all employees at all times.

It is the management's responsibility to see that every employee at *(the Facility)* is provided with safe working conditions, that all safety regulations are observed, and that employees use good common sense to protect themselves as well as others. A senior management representative will periodically inspect working conditions and may suggest changes in the safety policy accordingly. This representative will interface with a non-management representative (your elected SA8000 representative) to respond to your suggestions, questions, or concerns.

In addition, it is our policy to provide clean lavatories, access to potable and safe drinking water, and sanitary facilities for food storage. If dormitories are on-site, it is also our policy to ensure clean, safe dormitory facilities and to see that these facilities meet the basic needs of our employees.

Safety training

Every new employee at *(the Facility)* will be trained in our safety policy. This training will be repeated on a regular basis, at least once per year. [*SA8000 requires regular training to refresh the knowledge base of all employees.*]

Reporting injuries and accidents

Employees must advise their supervisor of all accidents, injuries, or illnesses that occur in the workplace. All accidents, injuries, or illnesses that occur while at work must be reported immediately, no matter how slight they may appear.

Accident report forms are available from your supervisor or from your safety representative. These are to be used for job-related accidents, injuries, and illnesses. (See sample below.)

A list of personnel trained in emergency procedures, such as basic first aid and CPR (cardio-pulmonary resuscitation) is posted in *(location)*. Please obtain assistance from them first. If outside medical assistance is needed, you should consult your health and safety representative whenever possible. If he or she is not available, then refer to the emergency phone number posted in *(location)*.

First aid kit

First aid supply kits are provided in the work area. It is the responsibility of the safety representative to see that the kits are well stocked. At the minimum, each kit should contain the following supplies: _____

_____

_____

Fire prevention

Fire extinguishers are located in the following places: _____ .

Each employee will receive instruction in their use during their initial safety training and in subsequent training sessions. If, at any time, you need to be retrained in their use, please consult your safety representative.

It is the responsibility of all employees to practice good housekeeping as part of our overall fire-prevention program. Keep your work area clean, fire exits clear and aisles free of clutter. Do not allow raw material, finished goods, or trash to be left in aisles or stairways.

Protective gear

When necessary, safety goggles or glasses will be provided by the company. Protective devices must be used at all times while working in the production areas of the plant, when handling hazardous materials and/or operating loud power tools and machinery.

Hearing protection devices are supplied by the company for jobs that require such devices. Employees must wear them if they are so instructed. Padded floors are also provided for those who stand at their jobs for most of the work-day. If any of these items are not available to you, please consult your safety representative.

Hazardous waste

[Note: This section is very US-specific, substitute appropriate regulatory references for your location.]

The US Environmental Protection Agency has grouped certain chemicals and chemical groups into categories which have been defined as toxic. This means that in concentrated forms or by accumulating and combining with other chemicals (even the air) these chemicals can be hazardous to human health if exposure occurs.

From time to time in the normal course of their jobs, employees may handle materials which have been classified as hazardous by the standards of the Occupational Safety and Health Act (OSHA) regulations.

Hazardous materials that are received from our suppliers should have Material Safety Data Sheets (MSDS) or labels which state the chemical ingredients of the contents, precautions to take, and what to do if exposure occurs.

If any employee suspects that the materials or waste he/she may encounter as an employee are hazardous (whether or not they are being created or used by the company), he/she should inform his/her supervisor or safety representative immediately.

As a company, we are committed to not creating or disposing of hazardous waste which will contaminate the environment. We will choose materials which have been judged as non-hazardous whenever possible and will properly dispose of hazardous materials if used. Also, we will not knowingly dump any waste into the environment at any time.

We will inform employees how to control hazardous waste and what to do if they are exposed to hazardous waste.

Figure 4.15 ■ **Accident report form**

Accident report form

Date _____

Name of injured employee_____

Name of manager on duty _____

Type of accident _____

Description of injury _____

Was protective gear in use at the time of accident? _____

Action(s) taken _____

Signatures:

Injured employee _____

Manager on duty _____

On-site nurse or doctor (if applicable) _____

Figure 4.16 ■ **Policy on freedom of association and the right to collective bargaining**

A. *(The Facility)* recognizes and respects the right of employees to freedom of association and collective bargaining. We will not tolerate any discrimination against trade union representatives, whether from management or co-workers. We will ensure that these representatives have open access to their members in the workplace.

B. In countries where this right is restricted under law: *(The Facility)* will see to it that parallel means of independent and free association and bargaining for all personnel are allowed. This means that we will respect the rights of all personnel to conduct separate, legal activities to achieve independent and free association and collective bargaining or any variation thereof on the premises.

Figure 4.17 ■ **Anti-discrimination policy**

At *(the Facility)*, there can be no discrimination in any conditions of employment including recruitment and hiring, opportunities for advancement, participation in training programs, wages, salaries, or benefits. Likewise, any form of discrimination by a supplier or subcontractor will not be tolerated.

All employees will be treated with respect and dignity. Any form of discrimination, such as that based on race, color, religion, national origin, sex, sexual orientation, age, marital status, or disability, by a supervisor or another employee will not be tolerated under any circumstances.

This policy also prohibits any form of harassment by supervisors, co-workers, or suppliers. It is not permissible to harass an employee because of his/her race, color, religion, national origin, sex, sexual orientation, age, marital status, or disability. This policy is intended to prohibit all offensive conduct, either physical or verbal, that threatens human dignity and employee morale, and which interferes with a positive and productive work environment.

The following are examples of the types of conduct that may constitute sexual harassment:

- physical assaults of a sexual nature, such as rape, sexual battery, molestation, or attempts to commit these assaults

- slurs, jokes or degrading comments, or unwanted attention of a sexual nature

- unwelcome sexual advances or flirtations

- suggestive or lewd remarks

- unwelcome hugging, touching, or kissing

- requests for sexual favors/propositions

- the display of sexually suggestive pictures or objects

- intentional physical contact or touching, such as patting, pinching, or brushing against another's body

- using sexually degrading words to describe an individual.

No employee will be retaliated against for protesting sexual overtures, refusing to submit to sexual advances, submitting to sexual advances, or raising a complaint concerning any violation of this harassment policy.

This policy prohibits any overt or subtle pressure for sexual favors, including implying or threatening that an applicant's or employee's co-operation of a sexual nature (or lack thereof) will have any effect on the person's employment, job assignment, wages, promotion, any other condition of employment, or future job opportunities.

Any employee who feels that he or she or another employee is a victim of harassment should immediately report the matter to his or her supervisor or to the facility manager. All complaints will be immediately recorded, investigated, and appropriate action will be taken.

(The Facility), where warranted, will take disciplinary action against any individual engaging in harassment. Depending on the circumstances, such disciplinary action may include suspension, demotion, or termination of employment. Disciplinary action will also be taken against those who make false allegations.

All reports of harassment will be kept confidential, limiting involvement only to those who have a need to know.

Figure 4.18 ■ Policy on disciplinary practices

(The Facility) will demonstrate respect at all times for employees' mental, physical, and emotional well-being. At no time will we condone the use of corporal punishment or other forms of mental or physical coercion; neither will we tolerate such behavior by our suppliers or subcontractors.

Figure 4.19 ■ Policy on working hours

Local law mandates a regular work week of no more than _____ hours, plus _____ hours of over-time, for a combined total of no more than _____ working hours in one seven-day period.

A. If local law allows a working week of **more than 48 hours**:

   (The Facility) permits a maximum working week of 48 hours, with over-time hours not to exceed 12 hours per week, for a combined total of 60 working hours in one seven day period.

B. If local law allows a working week of **48 hours or fewer:**

   (The Facility) permits a maximum working week of _____ hours, with over-time hours not to exceed 12 hours per week, for a combined total of _____ working hours in one seven-day period.

This policy ensures that all employees will have at least one day off in every seven-day period. Under normal business conditions, over-time work will be voluntary, and no employee will be permitted to exceed the maximum number of working hours per week. Only under short-term, exceptional business circumstances may we ask employees to work over-time. In all cases, all over-time hours (above 48) will be paid a premium rate of at least $1\frac{1}{2}$ times the regular rate. Under this policy, no homeworking will be allowed.

   In compliance with local law, all employees are entitled to a lunch break of _____ minutes and _____ additional breaks during the working day, each of _____ minutes. In addition, employees will be granted paid time off in the following manner: _____ sick days, _____ personal days, _____ vacation days, and these holidays:_____
_____.

Figure 4.20 ■ Compensation policy

Local law stipulates a minimum wage of _____ .
Industry standards in this region reflect a typical minimum wage of _____ .

   A basic needs assessment of this region indicates a minimum living wage to be _____ (sufficient to feed, clothe, and house a worker and his/her dependants from wages earned in a regular, 48-hour working week).

Employees at (*The Facility*) are compensated on an (*hourly or piecework*) basis, computed according to actual hours worked. These hours are recorded on either (your time card) (the sign-in/sign-out sheet). The pay rate begins at _____ , which has been established as the minimum living wage for a worker in a two-wage earning family and his/her dependants based on a 48-hour week. Incremental raises will be given based on level of experience, length of service, and performance reviews. Over-time pay begins after 48 hours of regular work in one week and will be calculated at 1½ times the regular rate.

Payroll will be issued (*frequency – day, time*) in the form of (check, cash, other). Certain benefits, such as (Social Security, federal income tax, unemployment insurance, disability insurance) will be deducted from each paycheck and will be itemized clearly on the accompanying paystub. Under no circumstances will paycheck deductions be made for disciplinary purposes. Any employee with questions about his/her paycheck should consult his/her supervisor for explanation or reconciliation.

Under certain circumstances, such as short-term training programs or apprenticeships, a lower than minimum wage may be established. These scenarios will be clearly defined ahead of time, with the training period not to exceed _____ weeks. Any employee in such a program who feels exploited or who has questions about the payment terms should bring these matters to the attention of his/her supervisor.

Figure 4.21 ■ Management systems policy document

The management of (*The Facility*) is committed to the policies described within this handbook. This includes a commitment to comply with all national and other applicable laws and to respect all applicable international conventions. We are also committed to a program of continual improvement.

We will make our best effort to document, implement, maintain, and communicate these policies to all appropriate personnel (employees, managers, supervisors, contractors, etc.). This information will be made available to the public upon request.

Management review

In carrying out this commitment, management will review on an annual basis the adequacy, suitability, and continuing effectiveness of the company's policies, including procedures and performance results against these policies. Amendments and improvements will be implemented where appropriate.

Company representative

(*The Facility*) has assigned _____ to serve as senior management representative, who will ensure that the requirements of these policies are met. Additionally, the company will provide for non-management personnel to choose a representative from their own group to facilitate communication with senior management on matters related to these policies.

Planning and implementation

(The Facility) will ensure that the requirements of these policies are understood and implemented at all levels of the company. This will include defining roles, responsibility and authority; training new and/or temporary employees; providing periodic training and awareness programs for existing employees; continuous monitoring of activities and results to demonstrate the effectiveness of systems implemented against the requirements of these policies.

Control of suppliers

(The Facility) will also establish and maintain appropriate procedures to evaluate and select suppliers based on their ability to meet the requirements of these policies. And we agree to maintain reasonable evidence that the requirements are being met by suppliers and subcontractors.

Addressing concerns and taking corrective action

(The Facility) will investigate, address, and respond to the concerns of employees and other interested parties with regard to conformance or non-conformance with the company's policies. No employee will be disciplined, dismissed, or otherwise discriminated against for providing information concerning observance of the policies. Depending on the nature and severity of any non-conformance identified against the company's policy, the company will implement remedial and corrective action and allocate adequate resources appropriately.

Outside communication

(The Facility) will establish and maintain procedures to communicate regularly to all interested parties information about its performance against these policies.

Access for verification

Where required by contract, *(The Facility)* will provide reasonable information and access to interested parties seeking to verify conformance to these policies. Similar access is expected of the company's suppliers and subcontractors.

Records

(The Facility) will maintain appropriate records to demonstrate conformance to these policies. Records will also be kept on subcontractors, including name, address, type and quantity of product supplied, and a registry of suppliers' social profiles.

Chapter 5 describes how to work with interested parties (IPs). The section contains a definition and provides context on each type of interested party. Keep in mind that interested parties vary greatly in size, in scope, and in outlook, and are influenced by many factors including region, political situation, and economic development. The chapter describes how IPs can help a company to introduce SA8000. The chapter concludes with case studies of best practice. Company managers should consider a local group in their region that may be of help and to take into account the various points in the chapter in relation to a specific IP. If you have trouble locating interested parties, use the Appendix or contact SAI.

5

Interested parties

Working with interested parties (IPs) is an essential part of implementing SA8000. There are many kinds of IPs: trade unions, non-governmental organizations (NGOs), business partners, competitors, the media, as well as government and international agencies. When welcomed as valuable participants, and shown a serious commitment to provide good conditions for workers, interested parties can become allies who assist companies in detecting and addressing problems. When ignored or treated as troublemakers, interested parties may raise problems in the media and with your customers. Consultation with IPs is a significant aspect of SA8000. This chapter provides an overview of the following issues.

- What are interested parties?
- How can companies identify which IPs to work with?
- How can companies develop partnerships with IPs?
- What are some of the challenges of working with IPs?
- Case studies of company-NGO involvement.

What are interested parties?

An interested party is: an individual or group concerned with or affected by the social performance of the company.

Interested parties are also known as "stakeholders," as they have a stake in the company. IPs include both local groups and local branches of global groups, including:

- human rights organizations
- community groups
- women's groups
- trade unions
- groups representing minorities
- groups representing children
- National Ministries of Labor
- consumer organizations
- development NGOs
- health workers
- labor lawyers and academics working on labor issues.

The term "stakeholder" is also used to define a broader range of parties, including consumers, shareholders, and suppliers. Chapter 7, on Communicating about SA8000, addresses how to communicate with consumers and other stakeholders on SA8000. Informing suppliers about SA8000 and promoting their participation in SA8000 is addressed in Chapter 4 on Implementation. This chapter focuses on the IPs that represent civil society with whom the company may at present have only limited awareness of and dialogue with. The Appendix lists a number of useful IP contacts. Certification firms also maintain a list of IPs.

Non-governmental organizations (NGOs)

NGOs are hard to define – in part because of the diverse roles they play and the varied nature of how they develop and operate. Even the term "non-governmental organization" is a poor term, defining the sector by what is it not. An NGO is a

"non-profit entity whose members are citizens or associations of citizens ... and whose activities are determined by the collective will of its members in response

to the needs of the members of one or more communities with which the NGO co-operates."[1]

Not all NGOs have "members"; "constituency" might be a better word.

NGOs play several important roles within the SA8000 framework, including:

- serving on the SAI Advisory Board;
- becoming accredited to conduct SA8000 audits;
- providing comments and advice on revisions of SA8000 and its *Guidance Document*;
- advising auditors on issues;
- filing complaints with certified facilities, certification bodies, and/or SAI;
- appealing the certification of a company or appealing the accreditation of a certification firm;[2]
- training workers on their rights and responsibilities under SA8000;
- educating the public; and
- accompanying auditors and participating in audits, where facilities agree.

Trade unions

As the official representative of workers, trade unions constitute one of the most important of the interested parties. Trade unions (TU) can be organized by sector, by geographic region, or by facility, and generally have the following structure:

Factory-level unions are known as the *Branch*.
Branches are represented at town/city level, known as the *District*.
Districts are represented at the regional level, known as the *Region*.
Representatives from all of the above constitute the *National Trade Union*.
Representatives from National Trade Unions affiliate to the *International Trade Secretariats*.

Facilities are divided into two categories: those that are organized and those that are not.

Because SA8000 auditors are encouraged to meet with trade union representatives at various levels, they can be helpful in providing contacts of key trade union officials. Implementation plans for SA8000 should be discussed with the facility's trade union officials. In some countries, trade unions are controlled by political parties or by the State (see Chapter 6 on Regional concerns). In such cases, the company implementing SA8000 will need to rely heavily on the non-management representative. However, even government-controlled unions may be helpful in providing a context on child labor and health and safety issues.

National Ministries of Labor

The National Ministries of Labor and their regional and municipal offices represent powerful allies in the implementation of SA8000. They serve as a source of information on regulations and changing legislation. These government bodies may also have inspectors who visit facilities, in which case there may already be a relationship with their office and a record and history of compliance. The labor inspectorates can play a major role in providing information on suppliers and in conducting risk assessment. Since SA8000 assists in promoting compliance with national legislation, Ministries of Labor can be helpful and important, even in countries with relatively weak democratic institutions.

SAI believes that the existence of SA8000 will help strengthen these national and municipal bodies, building their influence and reach. Under no circumstance should SA8000 be seen as a substitute for these governmental bodies. Rather, SA8000 complements the important work done by such governmental agencies.

Why are interested parties and NGOs so significant?

Interested parties have the potential to be allies in implementing SA8000 for several reasons: many NGOs understand the needs of the constituency they serve, having developed a sense of trust and credibility, while building expertise on issues related to SA8000. At the same time, they have the power to appeal a certification.

NGOs understand local needs

NGOs work closely with certain sectors within the community, giving them a sense of the pulse of the community, its concerns and aspirations.

NGOs have built **trust**

MANY NGOs HAVE BUILT A
SENSE OF TRUST WITHIN THE
COMMUNITY

Due to their close links to the community and to previous work to promote the community and its constituency, many NGOs have built a sense of trust within the community. Workers may share with an NGO or grass-roots group outside the facility concerns they may not voice within a facility.

NGOs have built **expertise**

Seek out IPs and NGOs that can provide companies with an overview of what the key problems are and how these might be addressed. A manager may wonder how to address the problem of child labor or of adult illiteracy. An NGO or IP can provide feedback on how to remediate children from the workplace, or how to provide literacy training to workers so that they may be able to read and follow health and safety standards. Hence, there is the potential for developing a partnership with NGOs in addressing common concerns.

NGOs deliver **services**

Some NGOs who deliver training, education, or health care can be important partners for companies seeking to implement SA8000. In a time when governments around the world are sharply reducing their expenditures on social projects, NGOs are becoming more powerful and can often deliver services with less bureaucracy than governments could in the past.

NGOs have **credibility**

Their services, expertise and the trust they engender endow NGOs with credibility. In many countries, especially where governments are highly bureaucratic and possibly corrupt, NGOs may be seen as the only real voice of the people. Working with NGOs helps to show workers that the company is serious about SA8000 and its implementation. But not all NGOs have developed credibility. As with any other type of organization, there may be problems of governance and abuse of power.

NGOs have the **power to appeal to revoke an SA8000 certification**

Some NGOs are antagonistic and anti-business and may work to promote awareness of abuses in the workplace. It is important for companies to engage in dialogue with such NGOs. While partnership with them is unlikely, face-to-face meetings can provide needed information. In such meetings, companies can alert the NGOs to the complaints and appeals procedures within SA8000. Dialogue is proof that there is a commitment to change and may prevent attacks against a company in the media. Establishing a constructive and ongoing dialogue ensures that, even if a company is cited in the media, the information is more likely to be accurate. The key thing to remember is to keep expectations realistic and to follow through on promises made. **NGOs and TUs are an integral part of SA8000 and companies ignore them at their peril.**

How can companies identify and select which IPs to work with?

Identifying interested parties (IPs) can be challenging in some regions of the world. Ideally, IPs should be representative and independent – yet in countries that are not democratic this could be difficult.

Because consultation with IPs can be time-consuming, it is important to select carefully which IPs to work with. How does a company select which IPs to work with? Obviously, the trade union representing the workers must be part of the consultation with IPs. But if the union is not a free union or is corrupt, then arrangements must also be made to meet with more representative worker groups. In areas where there are many IPs, it is useful to select the groups that are most representative of the workers and their families. The non-management representative can ask workers for indications of groups that they belong to or consider repre-sentative of their concerns.

Companies should be careful to examine the funding sources of NGOs. Are they funded by business? By political parties? Such funding could compromise their independence and neutrality. How transparent are these groups? Do they publish information on their funding sources? Their expenditures? Audits? To whom is the group accountable?

Selecting which IPs to work with should also be a function of the needs of the company. Different groups fulfill different goals. For example, which of the following types of "services" does your company most need from NGOs or other types of IPs?

- Information/advice
- Social services
- Funding for social projects for other NGOs
- Mediation
- Feedback
- Training.

Interested parties, such as NGOs, may have well-established guidelines about the kind of company they seek to work with. Oxfam, for example, has developed criteria for the type of company it will work with as follows.

- *"The company should have, or should be developing, a stated code of practice/statement of business ethics relating to how it sees its corporate responsibility.*
- *The implementation and monitoring of such statements should be included in the responsibilities of senior staff members, and reported to the board.*
- *Responsibility for on-the-ground implementation of such statements should be included in the duties of middle management to ensure their incorporation into the mainstream of the business.*
- *The company should be committed to transparency and openness, including independent external monitoring, or performance in the area of social responsibility.*
- *The company's senior management should be prepared to assume a public leadership role on the issue of corporate social responsibility."*[3]

While this list is geared towards multinational enterprises, it provides insight into how a major NGO views its relationship with companies. Just as companies are selective in choosing partners, so are IPs. Transparency and openness are fundamental to this process of dialogue between companies and IPs.

A company operating to SA8000 would necessarily meet all of the Oxfam criteria except the fifth, which requires the company to take a public leadership role on this issue. While SA8000 does not explicitly require companies to take a leadership role, the majority of SA8000 members and many SA8000 certified companies are doing so, working to raise awareness among other companies and governments.

How can companies develop relationships with NGOs?

Once an NGO has been identified, a company should share with it copies of SA8000 and request the NGO's views on what the major issues are for the community, for workers, and for minority groups. The latter groups are a bit tricky, as this constituency may be absent from the workplace, which could be a sign of exclusion. The company can also pose questions on how to address problems.

In some instances, developing trust will be a major concern; in other cases, the NGO will be pleased to be asked to play a role in improving working conditions. Fostering trust may be a challenge, as some NGOs may have a deep-seated distrust of companies. Building trust may take a considerable period of time. Companies working with NGOs report that, over time, the very process of inclusion can lessen tension. Excluding confrontational groups may only make them more confrontational. One suggestion for fostering trust is to offer the NGO a tour of the workplace. Demonstrating the efforts the company is making or those it plans to make to conform to SA8000 also demonstrates goodwill. The company should not provide special favors or expensive gifts to the NGO, for this may be considered a bribe and jeopardize the neutrality of the organization. If the NGO seeks a fee, then a contract should be agreed upon.

If there are many NGOs to consult with, companies may invite them as a group to talk with the company. Such broader sessions could generate new ideas, projects, and synergies. Whatever the format and size of the meetings, the focus should be on developing trust, listening to new perspectives, acquiring knowledge, and looking for synergies.

What are some of the challenges of working with NGOs?

"It is important to register the difference between debate and dialogue. Debate is unpredictable and takes place around positions. It may misinform and progress little.

Dialogue is managed, extremely responsive to participants' concerns, finds common ground, informs and provides a basis for moving forward."[4] Meetings and agendas are not enough, there is a need to foster a dialogue that leads to better understanding and enhanced communication.

If there has been no relationship between an NGO and the company, the first meeting(s) might be fraught with tension due to unresolved issues. The community's perception of the company may be based on out-dated information on conditions which the facility corrected in the process of becoming certified or preparing for certification. Emphasizing common interests will help to foster trust and build constructive dialogue.

While some NGOs may welcome dialogue, others do not.

"Steeped in a culture that encourages adversarial attitudes to the powers that be, many NGOs seem best suited to confrontation ..."[5]

Like any other type of organization, they may select priority issues based on what is most likely to get them funding or media coverage.

Companies should be careful not to generate high expectations that cannot be met. While there are areas where the company can help promote the NGO's interest, these should not be oversold, as such a scenario could lead to discord. Many NGOs, especially in the developing world, may represent disadvantaged groups whose needs are great and, consequently, so are their expectations. Providing direct funding to them could jeopardize their neutrality or that of the company. Other NGOs are comfortable with receiving funding from the corporate community and have developed special procedures to assure independence. There are several models that companies can follow in pursuing relationships with NGOs, some of which are presented in the case studies at the end of this chapter.

Working with NGOs may represent an entirely new endeavor for the company. Where such consultations have not occurred before, the list of concerns can be quite lengthy. It is important that companies listen to these concerns – even if they are unrelated to SA8000. Certain concerns may represent needs or issues that should be addressed in order to develop trust. Because of its leverage, a company may be able to help an IP by raising the concerns of a community with government officials, as in the case below of Hindustan Lever. Becoming a more inclusive company will facilitate the implementation of SA8000.

Among the most powerful type of coalitions are those that include many types of parties, representing a variety of constituencies. The Atlanta Agreement is an example of such a coalition, involving NGOs, the private sector, and UNICEF to promote education for children in the Sialkot region of Pakistan.

The Atlanta Agreement: a partnership to combat child labor in Pakistan

In the mid-1990s, the media began to expose the working conditions in the Sialkot region of Pakistan, with young children making soccer balls for famous brands. The Sialkot Chamber of Commerce fought back by forging the Atlanta Agreement, involving a commitment by large companies to avoid the use of child labor, while allowing inspections from the ILO. Child workers would be mainstreamed into schools with the assistance of several local IPs, including the local office of Save the Children. Sixty-six manufacturers, who together produce 90 percent of the exports of the region, have teamed up to combat child labor. Today, there is "almost zero child labor," according to a Save the Children representative in the region. Six thousand children are in schools managed by partner groups. Local schools have been improved.[6]

The manufacturers code the balls, to facilitate tracking them through the supply chain. This has led manufacturers to have greater control of the supply chain and to operate more efficiently. On-time deliveries have increased as a result of better tracking from 50–80 percent.[7]

However, implementing change in Sialkot comes with a price. Overall family income has fallen by approximately 20 percent, as children enter the schools and women have lost earning power, for their religion forbids them to work in the stitching centers created to facilitate inspections.[8]

To combat the adverse side effects of its actions, the ILO is creating small stitching centers that employ as few as three women, which does not violate the cultural practice of the region. One IP provides small loans to families so that they can start up small businesses to replace lost earnings.

This case study illustrates the advantages of working with the Chamber of Commerce, an entity able to mobilize a large number of companies within a sector, all of whom face similar issues. The Sialkot region also demonstrates how addressing one social issue (child labor) can exacerbate problems in another arena (women's opportunities and family earnings).

Centro Nuovo Modelo di Sviluppo and the Appeals Process

In late 1999, the Centro Nuovo Modelo di Sviluppo, an Italian NGO, found evidence that a supplier to a certified company in Kenya was violating SA8000. The Centro took their complaint to an Italian food company that owned and operated this Kenyan facility, but was ignored. Afterwards, the Centro notified Co-op Italia, a buyer. Co-op Italia promptly took action, triggering a dialogue between the NGO, the company, and a certification firm that Co-op Italia had engaged to audit its private label suppliers. Two certification bodies then audited the facility and brought together interested parties for discussion. The Kenyan company agreed to take action on the Corrective Action Requests (CARs) issued.

This case study demonstrates how NGOs are aware of abuses and will bring them to the attention of certified facilities and company management through the SA8000 complaints system. Had SA8000 not been in place, there would have been no mechanism for such a dialogue. This case also demonstrates how global NGOs have become. An Italian NGO is able to glean information about abuses in Africa and report them to a certified customer of the facility's management and to SAI. The message is clear: NGOs and other IPs are able to discover problems and use SA8000 to press for social change.

Working with IPs and NGOs may require companies "to think outside the box," to use a decidedly American expression. The case of Hindustan Lever is an example of a company taking creative measures to address business as well as social concerns. While this case study is not directly related to SA8000, it does demonstrate the need for long-term, creative approaches for companies operating in poor, rural communities.

Hindustan Lever

A subsidiary of Unilever, Hindustan Lever operated an unsuccessful dairy in a rural part of India. Before deciding to cut its losses by shutting down the dairy, the company tried to address the reason for the failure of its business: poverty. It used its influence with the government to seek funding for roads and schools in the remote region of Uttar Pradesh, where the dairy was located. The company invested in the community, providing loans to farmers so that they could improve the health of their cows, which in turn generated better quality milk and in greater quantities. Promoting infrastructure and development allowed the dairy to remain operational.[9]

The lesson for companies implementing SA8000 is that the leverage of the private sector can generate funding from governments. A company that can think outside the box might provide the momentum to generate awareness and funding from international and/or multilateral organizations. Companies can also consider working in partnership with other local companies or with their major customers, who may have a greater global profile.

Chapter 6 serves as a reference and can be used to check issues for specific geographic regions. For each region, several key issues have been chosen as representing some of the most serious issues. Clearly, entire volumes exist on each region or on specific countries, providing extensive background. The goal of this section is to provide an overview of major regions to illustrate that all regions face serious problems. This section can be useful for companies conducting a risk analysis of their supply chain. Each region also includes some country information, for which the name of the country appears in italic type. The reader is advised that there are differences in how each region is presented; this is due partly to the fact that SAI's regional workshops took place only in three regions, so there is more information for Asia, Latin America, and Eastern Europe, than there is for North America, Western Europe, and Africa.

6

Regional concerns

SA8000 is a global standard that is operational around the world. There is a common misperception that only the South, or developing countries, can benefit from the implementation of SA8000. The reality is that the industrialized North also stands to gain from the adoption of SA8000. There are significant abuses of workers' rights in the industrialized countries, as well as in the developing world. Immigrants in world capitals such as New York City and London, who don't speak the local language or know their legal rights, are subject to exploitation, just as they might be in their home countries, often with very little recourse. Migrants also face significant exploitation, especially if they are illegal. However, several characteristics of developing countries make workers in the South more vulnerable: the lack of enforcement of labor laws, the high concentration of economic activity that is informal, the prevalence of corruption, and high rates of poverty.

In implementing SA8000, it is important to understand the regional issues that may affect implementation. Regional difficulties, however, cannot be used as an excuse for overlooking elements of the standard. SA8000 must be applied as a whole, regardless of location. Each region presents its own challenges to implementation.

Regional differences are a result of several factors, with cultural differences playing an important role. SA8000, as a global standard, does not intend to ignore or erode cultural practice. For example, religious norms and laws in some Muslim countries require that men and women work separately. Segregated factories would not violate SA8000, unless the women earn less than men, work under conditions that are less safe, or are offered fewer opportunities for advancement.

This chapter addresses current trends in six major regions: Asia, Latin America, Africa, Eastern Europe, Western Europe, and North America. While reading this chapter, it is important to remember that each region, country, and municipality has its own unique profile that generalizations cannot convey. Working conditions also vary dramatically according to sector. Conditions in companies producing for the export market may vary dramatically from those producing for the local market. The same factory may, alternately, produce for both markets. However, several trends do emerge at both the regional and national levels that can provide guidance to companies developing strategies for implementing SA8000 and for companies conducting risk analysis of their supplier base. This chapter is based, in part, on three regional consultations organized by SAI in partnerships with local NGOs that took place in Brazil, the Philippines, and in Hungary during 1999–2000.

REGIONAL DIFFICULTIES, HOWEVER, CANNOT BE USED AS AN EXCUSE FOR OVERLOOKING ELEMENTS OF THE STANDARD

In reading this section, keep in mind that entire volumes have been written on the employment and social conditions in each region. The snapshots provided in each section should serve to provide a glimpse of the complexities of applying SA8000 under diverse regional scenarios. The regional differences also serve to emphasize the need for hiring local managers, auditors, and consultants who understand local regulations, culture, and best practice. As it is hard to do justice to the complexities of each region and sector, SAI urges the readers to seek further information in the *Guidance Document* and the training sessions, while also consulting the reference materials listed in the Appendix. SAI is planning to expand the training sessions to include an extra segment on local concerns.

■ Asia

In many Asian countries, the economic crisis has led to a deterioration of working conditions. The rise in unemployment has made people more likely to consider jobs where conditions may be poor. A number of Asian countries, including *China*, *Singapore*, and *Malaysia*, have argued that the concept of human rights discussed in the West is fundamentally different from the notion of human rights in Asia. In many fora, including the United Nations, the case has been made that human rights in the West centers around the rights of the individual, whereas the Asian focus is on the rights of the community.

In August 1999, SAI hosted a consultative workshop in Quezon City, the Philippines, with several partners, including the Trade Union Congress of the Phillipines, the International Textile, Garment and Leather Workers' Federation, and the Philippine Business for Social Progress. Below is an excerpt of the meeting's key points.[1]

Workshop report

All nine elements of the standard are deemed significant to the current working conditions and practices in Southeast Asia. Some elements, however, are considered more relevant than others to the region. These elements have been identified as follows.

Freedom of association and collective bargaining

A relatively high percentage of workers remain non-unionized in the region. Many companies distrust organized labor, and have employed strategies that prevent their workers from forming unions. In the *Philippines*, for instance, laws on workers' rights on free association are well established, but companies have taken advantage of legal complexities to derail their workers' attempts at forming unions. Other companies continue practices such as employing workers with contracts that end just before they are entitled to start receiving benefits from the company. Some government officials have collaborated with business to prevent organized labor from penetrating (export) processing zones ....

Some unions exist in name only; they are controlled either by their companies or by the State, as in the case of *Thailand*, *Vietnam*, and *China* for instance. Whether the worker decides for or against joining a union, the State retains its control over his/her rights as a worker.

▶

Child labor

Child labor is widely practiced in the region, especially in small, sometimes home-based, enterprises. Children as young as … seven are employed to do adult work, often under exploitative terms and in inhumane working conditions. This has become a major issue in Thailand, for instance, where child laborers are suspected of working in prison-like circumstances because of the employers' fear of exposure. Poverty and the difficulty of meeting basic needs have driven parents to use their children to help augment the family income. Governments have done little to halt the practice.

The few attempts at monitoring and checking child labor have been largely carried out by NGOs, international funding agencies, and organized labor. The small sizes of subcontractors' facilities and their location in the entire supply chain have constrained monitoring efforts ….

Forced labor

Child laborers are often forced by their own parents to work, instead of exercising their right to education. The children themselves, often because of cultural traditions that prohibit children to disobey their parents, are powerless against their parents. Children, however, are not the only victims of forced labor. There have been documented cases of prisoners, women, and migrant workers being subjected to the same practice. Like child laborers, they are made to work under wretched working conditions often on exploitative terms. (The problem of forced labor in *Myanmar*, formerly *Burma*, is so serious that it has caused boycotts of companies operating there.)

Discrimination

Most employers in the region prefer to employ workers of a particular sex or religion or ethnic group, often regardless of the latter's qualifications. The practice has to do mainly with cultural values and traditions associated with particular groups of people. Traditional male-female roles, for instance, dictate that women are assigned certain types of work which are different from those given to men. Shoemart, the largest chain of department stores in the *Philippines*, prefers to employ applicants who are members of *Iglesia ni Cristo* because this sect does not allow its members to organize unions. In *Vietnam*, where "regionalism" is prevalent, employers prefer to employ workers from one place over equally qualified workers coming from other places.

Child labor statistics

While it is impossible to address the experience of each Asian nation, it is helpful to provide statistics on child labor in some of the key exporting countries in the region. The extent of child labor can serve as a useful barometer for other issues, including wages.

Figure 6.1 ■ Child labor in Asia

Country	Population in millions (1996)	Age range	Children in age range who work (%)
Bangladesh	122	5–14	19.1
India	945	5–14	5.4
Pakistan	134	5–14	8.0
Philippines	72	5–14	10.6
Thailand	60	10–14	16.2

Source: US Department of Labor (1998) *By the Sweat and Toil of Children*, V, 14.

▨ Latin America

The trend towards regional trade blocs has led to greater interest in workers rights throughout Latin America. In *Mexico*, the debate over labor rights and human rights intensified during the negotiations and implementation of the North American Free Trade Agreement (NAFTA), with several new NGOs created in Mexico to focus on working conditions. During the MERCOSUR (the Southern Cone Free Trade Agreement between *Brazil, Argentina, Paraguay,* and *Uruguay*) there were tri-partite negotiations about codes of conduct. The metal workers sector was able to make the most progress. The leather, textile, shoe, and civil construction sectors also discussed codes of conduct.

The term *maquiladora*, used to describe factories along the US–Mexico border, has become synonymous with factories throughout Latin America with poor working conditions. In these assembly plants, young women produce clothing, shoes, and electronic goods for export. While working conditions are often poor in these factories, competition is often fierce for such jobs.

Latin America faces serious social problems, including poverty, the rights of indigenous peoples, and the access to land for the poor. These serious social issues are not included in SA8000, but are very significant issues which need to be addressed by companies, such as those that own vast tracts of land which may be contested by indigenous groups. These issues may cause problems with NGOs or other interested parties which may make it more difficult for companies to establish good relationships with interested parties.

As in many other regions of the world, Latin American nations often have excellent labor laws, but these are rarely enforced consistently. The existence of laws, however, does provide a good starting point for discussions with suppliers. The existence of a large informal sector also poses problems for implementing SA8000, as auditors require data and systems to certify compliance.

In June 1999, SAI organized a workshop on SA8000 in Latin America, with several co-sponsors, including IBASE, Instituto Ethos, and Connexão. One of the most interesting aspects of the tri-partite workshop was that representatives from trade unions, NGOs, and companies had very little contact with one another prior to the meeting. There was keen interest among the three sectors to work to promote SA8000 throughout Latin America.

The key issues for Latin America are as follows.

Wages

The minimum wage in many regions of Latin America does not provide for basic needs. Devaluations and high rates of inflation erode earning power, while high rates of unemployment also place downward pressure on wages. The Interfaith Center for Corporate Responsibility (ICCR) and the Coalition for Justice in the Maquiladoras have conducted studies in 12 cities in the *maquiladora* sector in Mexico. According to David Schilling of the ICCR,

"there is a big difference between what companies are paying workers and what they need to support themselves and their families."[2]

Discrimination

Gender-based discrimination is a serious problem throughout Latin America. Given the high concentration of young female workers in assembly plants, there is concern over how employers deal with women who become pregnant and who are pregnant at the time of applying for work. Several union representatives report cases of women who are forced to take birth control pills or who are fired upon becoming pregnant, so that the company can avoid paying them maternity benefits. Human Rights Watch documents a pattern of discrimination against pregnant women in *Mexico*.[3] Discriminating against pregnant workers, in hiring or firing, violates SA8000, as it constitutes a form of gender-based discrimination.

Freedom of association

Many suppliers to major global brands have taken measures to bar workers from unionizing. Threatened with the loss of their jobs, many workers resist joining unions. These problems are particularly serious in *Central America*. There are reports that in many free-trade zones, workers affiliated with unions are blacklisted. In *Mexico*, trade unions are controlled by the government and lack independence.

Child labor

Child labor is a serious problem in many Latin American countries due to high rates of poverty and to a very young population. Rates of child labor in *Central America* are growing, with serious abuses in the agricultural sector.[4]

Figure 6.2 ■ **Child labor in Latin America**

Country	Total population in millions (1996)	Age range	Children in age range who work (%)
Brazil	161	5–14	19
Guatemala	11	7–14	4.1
Mexico	93	12–14	17.3
Nicaragua	5	10–14	9.9
Peru	24	6–14	4.1

Source: US Department of Labor (1998) *By the Sweat and Toil of Children*, V, 14.

Africa

Several African countries are part of the complex supply chain of major companies working on SA8000. Companies are relying more on *Egypt* and *Tunisia* for contract production. *South Africa* has a significant export market. Countries such as *Zimbabwe* and *Kenya* provide agricultural produce for many European supermarkets. While Africa, as a continent, does not have the high levels of trade with the US and Europe that Asia and Latin America enjoy, the region faces severe, often crippling, social problems that make the adoption of SA8000 a priority. Among the social problems in the region are poverty, hunger, and the scourge of AIDS.

In Fig. 6.3 one can see that a significant percentage of the children in *Kenya* and *Tanzania* work.

Figure 6.3 ▪ Child labor in Africa[5]

Country	Total population in millions (1996)	Age range	Children in age range who work (%)
Egypt	59	6–14	12
Kenya	27	10–14	41.3
South Africa	38	10–14	4.2
Tanzania	30	10–14	39.5

Source: US Department of Labor (1998) *By the Sweat and Toil of Children*, V, 14.

The AIDS pandemic has created unparalleled social crisis, slowly eroding progress previously made in education and life expectancy, with dramatic consequences for the workplace. According to UNAIDS, the number of AIDS orphans is estimated at 13.2 million in Sub-Saharan Africa alone, with the number projected to rise to 42 million by 2010.[6]

THE AIDS PANDEMIC HAS CREATED UNPARALLELED SOCIAL CRISIS, SLOWLY ERODING PROGRESS PREVIOUSLY MADE IN EDUCATION AND LFIE EXPECTANCY, WITH DRAMATIC CONSEQUENCES FOR THE WORKPLACE

With the rising toll of AIDS deaths, many companies are faced with a grim problem: how to deal with sick employees and the AIDS orphans of their former employees. In some cases, companies are hiring the AIDS orphans of their former employees, providing them with shelter, income, and food. A European supermarket chain has suppliers who are employing such orphans in *Zimbabwe*. The AIDS crisis raises tough issues for SA8000. Is it possible to provide remediation for such children? As always, the focus should be on improving the lives and well-being of the children. With scant assistance from the government, coalitions of interested parties are necessary to address this complex and tragic issue. In some countries, such as *Mauritius*, there are no labor laws, nor is there a minimum wage. According to Heather White of Verite, codes of conduct offer the only level of protection available to workers in such countries.[7]

A key issue for Africa, as with other developing regions, is the existence of a large informal economy, often vibrant, but unregulated. In *Senegal*, fewer than 30 percent of the urban population are employed within the formal sector.[8] In factories operating in the informal sector, it is less likely that companies maintain data and comply with legislation.

While SAI has not yet sponsored a workshop in Africa, a certification firm has sponsored awareness sessions on the standard in Morocco.

■ Eastern Europe

There are a number of issues which SA8000 could help to address in Eastern Europe as follows.

Discrimination

"Ethnic and age discrimination ... (are) significant in the CEE (Central and Eastern European) context. For example, Roma (Gypsies) are routinely discriminated against in hiring, and migrant labor from poorer countries in Southeastern Europe, such as Romania and Bulgaria, to wealthier neighbors in the region, such as Hungary and the Czech Republic, is also creating tension in this area. Age discrimination has become a problem in the 'New Economy', as older workers have not been able to benefit from new opportunities due to outmoded skills, the lack of foreign language training, etc"[9]

Wages

There is a downward pressure on wages and working conditions as the region seeks to compete with other regions. In addition, wages tend to be under-reported. This makes adherence to a standard such as SA8000 more complex.

Eastern Europe is seeking management expertise to redesign and develop the face of its industry. As a result, ISO standards are becoming increasingly popular. The implementation of such standards will facilitate the implementation of SA8000.

Eastern European workshop on SA8000

In March 2000, SAI and several Eastern European groups hosted a workshop on SA8000. The local partners included the Center for Business Ethics, The Budapest University of Economic Sciences, Hungary and the Business Ethics Centre, The Institute of Philosophy and Sociology, Polish Academy of Sciences, and the L. Kozminski Academy of Entrepreneurship and Management, Poland.

Workshop summary

A considerable part of the meeting was devoted to exploring the impact of the region's political, social, and economic transitions on corporate social responsibility and workplace relations. Among the concerns expressed by participants were the weak social safety net (compared to the communist period) and the disparity between the public perception of the State role in social protection, versus the State's current capacity to fulfill these functions.

There is considerable variation in economic and social development within CEE countries. Conditions for workers are generally considered to be significantly worse in *Bulgaria* and *Romania*, where homeworking and abuses in the textile and garment industry occur. Such practices are much less frequent in neighboring *Poland*, *Hungary*, and the *Czech Republic* and *Slovakia*.

Central and Eastern Europe have comparatively high level of labor standards, which according to Dr Giuseppe Casale, the acting director of the ILO, are better than in other regions. Although countries in the region have ratified many of the ILO core conventions, problems still exist in achieving effective implementation of the same. This is where private voluntary initiatives can help, not just in implementation, but also in the enforcement of the core labor standards.

Many governments are under pressure to weaken labor laws and this results in downward pressure on the minimum wage and other working conditions. This is especially true in *Bulgaria*, where workers face poor working conditions and low wages, especially among women garment workers.

Multinational companies in *Hungary* have created new jobs and implemented better environmental practices, but at the same time problems with trade union rights have increased. *Hungary* has an extensive black market. SA8000, in attempting to formalize workplaces, could address this issue.

Trade union membership is decreasing in *Poland*, according to Mr Ryzard Lepik, Vice-President of the Polish trade union OPZZ.[10] The OPZZ is working on several levels, including the non-traditional role of protecting workers and their families' rights; they see this multi-leveled approach as key.

■ Western Europe

With dwindling birth rates, Western Europe is heavily reliant on workers from outside the region. High rates of poverty and unemployment throughout the world make employment in the region desirable, despite barriers to entry. United for Intercultural Action, a Dutch organization, estimates that more than 2,000 refugees and migrants have died trying to enter the European Union.[11]

The key issues for Western Europe are as follows.

Wages

Sweatshops exist in major European cities such as London, just as they do in other large urban centers. While these workplaces are not the norm, they do pose serious issues, such as wages, health and safety problems, over-time.

Health and safety

Companies seeking to adopt SA8000 is Europe are finding that routine health and safety concerns are sometimes ignored.

Child labor

In *Italy*, child labor and wages are expected to be problematic – given the influx of migrants from Eastern Europe. Italy has passed legislation stating that SA8000 certification will satisfy its requirements to combat child labor.

North America

To rephrase Gertrude Stein's words,[12] a sweatshop is a sweatshop is a sweatshop. Characterized by low wages and poor conditions, these workplaces are prevalent around the world due to the ease of start-up. Anyone with a few sewing machines can produce garments, often as part of the informal economy. These types of businesses often operate with complete disregard to labor legislation. Many abuses of SA8000 occur in large metropolitan centers, such as New York and Los Angeles, where illegal immigrants agree to work in sweatshops because they have no legal recourse. Several cases of forced labor have been reported in US cities. Use of migrant labor is common in harvesting of fruits and vegetables and poses several problems.

There is evidence that compliance with local and federal legislation is falling. Only a third of the clothing manufacturers in Los Angeles were found to be in compliance with legislation. Two years ago, 39 percent were not in compliance.[13]

According to Human Rights Watch, there are hundreds of thousands of child workers involved in the agricultural sector in the US, many of whom are exposed to serious health and safety problems, such as pesticide poisoning and heat illness. Over-time is also a problem, with many youths unable to attend school due to the long work-days, often as long as 12 to 14 hours per day. US law exempts farmworker youth from age and hour requirements.[14]

The right to organize in the US is coming under closer scrutiny. According to statistics from the National Labor Relations Board (NLRB) (a US Government agency), more workers are being fired for trying to organize trade unions than in previous years. In the 1990s, there were 20,000 such cases per year, compared with only 6000 in 1969.[15] The NLRB issues remedial orders when such cases are found.

"Human Rights Watch found that one-sided rules for union organizing unfairly favor employers over workers. Farm workers, domestic workers, low-level supervisors, and other categories of workers are expressly denied labor-law protection for organizing and basic rights. Immigrants especially face discrimination."[16]

Chapter 7 provides information on how to communicate with stakeholders and disclose information about compliance with SA8000. While there are concrete measures member companies need to take, the reader is advised to be creative in devising a communications strategy. The manner in which you communicate is influenced by the culture of the company and the culture in which it operates. Keep in mind that communications includes strategy, goals, and targets, it is how stakeholders can hold a company accountable. This information will serve as a guide to other companies seeking to develop SA8000 management systems. Communicating about the kinds of corrective actions taken at facilities will go a long way to convince skeptics about the ability of codes of conduct to improve the quality of life for people around the world.

7

Communicating about SA8000

"Disclosure is important because it will drive companies to improve in order to show better numbers over time."

Simon Billenness, Trillium Asset Management[1]

SA8000 provision

SA8000 9.11 *The company shall establish and maintain procedures to communicate regularly to all interested parties data and other information regarding performance against the requirements of this document, including, but not limited to, the results of management reviews and monitoring activities.*

Communication is an integral part of SA8000. Communication will increase awareness of SA8000 and hold companies accountable to their key stakeholders: consumers, shareholders, suppliers, NGOs, and unions. The challenge is for companies to provide information that is timely and relevant to their stakeholders, without inundating them with data.

A second challenge is to make the information accessible to an appropriate range of stakeholders. For global companies, these stakeholders may be located around the world, speaking many different languages and with different levels of literacy. Access to different types of media and computers will also differ from country to country and stakeholder to stakeholder.

It is important to differentiate between disclosing and communicating. Disclosure implies a one-way flow of data from the company to the stakeholder, whereas communication is a two-way flow of information from the company to the stakeholder and back. Both disclosure and communication are essential to the SA8000 system.

A communications strategy on SA8000 needs to consider the following questions.

- What type of information needs to be disclosed?
- To whom?
- In what form?
- To what end?
- Who verifies this information and how?
- How can disclosure lead to communication?

This chapter answers these questions, while providing case studies of how companies are communicating about SA8000.

What type of information needs to be disclosed to the public?

There are three groups which need to disclose:

- signatory members
- SA8000 applicants
- SA8000 certified suppliers.

Each group has somewhat different aims and audiences. However, all three groups need to emphasize:

- objectives and goals
- corrective actions (CAs) or real improvements made
- performance to date
- verification
- benefits to the company and the community.

SAI has stipulated that SA8000 signatory members should communicate to its suppliers (as defined in SA8000) and its own production facility managers the following.

- A policy that conformance to SA8000 is expected for its suppliers and its own production facilities.

- Notification that SA8000 Certified and Applicant Suppliers will immediately be given preference, with a greater preference for Certified Suppliers.

- Notification of specified dates by which SA8000 Applications and SA8000 Certification will become a contractual obligation for the SA8000 signatory member's suppliers and / or a requirement for its own production facilities.

Signatory membership renewal, year II

The SA8000 signatory member has established a management system to implement its SA8000 policy. Expectations, communications, and the management system shall be in place to qualify for year II renewal of Signatory Membership.

Signatory member reports

The SA8000 signatory member shall disclose to the public, on an annual basis, the following independently verified information.

SA8000 applicants

- The number of its suppliers and its own production facilities that have attained SA8000 applicant status at the end of the report year (and, as applicable, for the previous year and cumulative).

- For comparison, the number of SA8000 applicants set as an objective by the signatory member company for the report year.

- The number of SA8000 applicants set as an objective by the signatory member company for the forthcoming year(s).

SA8000 certified suppliers

- The number of its suppliers and its own production facilities that are currently certified for compliance with SA8000 at the end of the report year (and, as applicable, for the previous year and cumulative).

- For comparison, the number of SA8000 certified suppliers and production facilities set as an objective by the signatory member company for the report year.

- The number of SA8000 certified suppliers and facilities set as an objective by the signatory member for the forthcoming year(s).

Universe of suppliers

- The signatory member's universe of suppliers, e.g. the approximate number of suppliers each year. The number can be expressed in rounded numbers or as a range.

Optional information

The SA8000 signatory member *may and is encouraged, but not required*, to also disclose one or more of the following.

- A description of the types and approximate numbers of corrective actions implemented, by geographic region and, if significant, by industrial sector, as a result of:
  - the SA8000 signatory member's first or second party monitoring; and/or
  - third party accredited certification body certification audits.
- The names of its SA8000 certified suppliers.
- A list of its suppliers and its own production facilities.
- The proportion of suppliers that are SA8000 applicants and/or certified by volume.

Signatory membership renewal, year III

A *verified* SA8000 signatory member report must be issued in order to qualify for year III of signatory membership, and annually for subsequent signatory membership renewals. Verification of SA8000 signatory member reports will be performed by SAI. SAI shall pilot, develop, and submit to the Advisory Board proposed systems for verification.

SA8000 members must report the number of suppliers they have, expressed either as a rounded number or as a range.

SA8000 members are also encouraged to report the following type of information:

- a description of the types of and approximate numbers of corrective actions implemented by region and industrial sector;

- the names of its SA8000-certified suppliers;
- a list of its suppliers and its own production facilities; and
- the proportion of suppliers that are SA8000 applicants and/or certified by volume.

After three years as an SA8000 member, a company must publish an SA8000 report. This report must be verified by SAI. This information will be made available on the SAI website.

Communication with suppliers

Communication with *suppliers* needs to include:

- a policy that conforms to SA8000;
- notification that SA8000 certified and applicant suppliers will immediately be given preference, with a higher preference allocated to certified suppliers; and
- notification of specified dates by which SA8000 application and SA8000 certification will become a contractual obligation.

What form can the communication take?

Communicating about SA8000 is similar to the ISO model. While no label is placed on goods produced in a certified facility, the company may display their certificate on letterhead, on trucks or vehicles, in reports, and on plaques in their facility or stores.

Companies working to SA8000 are also speaking about SA8000 at conferences and workshops, when meeting with industry organizations and at trade meetings to promote the standard and better working conditions.

What are the benefits of communication?

There are many benefits of communicating your company's commitment to SA8000. The SA8000 certificate provides an assurance that your company produces goods under safe and fair conditions, as stipulated by the community of nations through the conventions of the International Labour Organization. A report allows you to explain to interested parties what the SA8000 certificate means to your business. The report provides an opportunity for publicizing the positive impact of certification on the bottom line, including employee morale and retention, productivity, and quality.

There are business benefits to disclosure as well. Should allegations or criticisms be made, a public report puts your company on the record. Consumers respect genuine efforts and improvements more than bland statements of principle. Above all, disclosure leads to enhanced performance, as companies measure and track progress, they are able to set goals and targets which lead to greater social accountability.

How does disclosure lead to communication?

Disclosing your company's commitment to and adoption of SA8000 facilitates communication with interested parties. Through disclosure, stakeholders become aware of a company's commitments to improve over time. Once objectives are set and reported, a company may need the assistance of interested parties to meet its targets.

Disclosure provides a window into the activities of the company, allowing for greater transparency, a prerequisite for accountability. In order to hold companies accountable, interested parties must have information on what is happening within the walls of the company. On-going disclosure of progress on the social front helps to build trust among interested parties, facilitating compliance with SA8000.

Best practice in social reporting

Companies seeking to produce reports on social issues have two excellent guides to follow: Accountability 1000 and the Global Reporting Initiative.

AccountAbility 1000 (AA1000)

This is a standard for companies seeking to communicate with stakeholders. AA1000 is a process standard – it specifies a process rather than defining performance, as SA8000 does. Launched in November 1999 by the Institute for Social and Ethical Accountability, AA1000 details how companies can hold discussions with stakeholders and how they can communicate findings to the public. The standard encompasses sourcing issues, but also addresses a wide range of other issues important to stakeholders, from environment to animal welfare. A company could integrate AA1000 and SA8000 by using the AA1000 model to communicate with interested parties on issues relating to workers' rights and publish a report which met AA1000 guidelines on SA8000 compliance.

AA1000 recommends that social reports should set targets and objectives. (SA8000 is an example of a set of targets and objectives.) This allows for tracking trends over time. When a second report is issued, it should describe performance based on targets set in the previous report. Has the company met its objectives? If not, why not? If so, how? If exceeded, how? AA1000 also encourages companies to publish comments from stakeholders on the company's progress. The goal is information that is

"inclusive, complete, material, comparable, reliable, relevant, and understandable."[2]

A useful tool for assuring continuous improvement is to request feedback from interested parties. The feedback is then integrated into the development of future reports, ensuring that disclosure leads to communication. For example – a company can discuss with key interested parties whether the information meets their needs.

Global Reporting Initiative

The *Global Reporting Initiative* (GRI) is in the process of developing and piloting a common framework for reporting. GRI provides formats, issues, and indicators for reports, while reporting on stakeholder relationships. GRI has issued draft rules on environmental issues and is in the process of developing social criteria. A wide range of companies are piloting the GRI model. In the future, SAI will seek to pilot GRI reporting and AA1000 with SA8000 member companies.

Chapter 8 – while none of us has a crystal ball, it is possible to examine current trends and to project their importance into the future. In interviews with key players in the SA8000 community and beyond, few people dared make a projection about the future. Keep in mind that there is a significant degree of uncertainty, magnified by the dynamic state of this field.

8

The future of SA8000

"In five years, we hope that SA8000 has the same standing as ISO9000 has now. In ten years, we hope that most of our foreign suppliers are certified."[1]

Jouko Kuisma, Kesko, Finland

"We think that SA8000 is going to become more popular among consumers in the next five years."[2]

Marisa Parmigiani, SMAER, an Italian consulting firm to Co-op Italia

What does an SA8000 world look like? Workplaces will become more free and fair. Companies will forge stronger partnerships with their suppliers, while taking a more inclusive approach with interested parties. Beyond these direct consequences, there are other interesting trends taking place which both affect and are affected by SA8000. This chapter presents a vision for the future, involving the following elements:

- combined and integrated audits, linking social concerns to the environment and quality;
- convergence with existing social standards;
- improving the SA8000 system;

- the challenge of partnership;
- the rise of a hybrid auditor;
- new legislation.

Integrated audits: the holy grail of the auditing world[3]

Despite widespread agreement that social and environmental issues are inextricably linked, auditing of these issues continues to take place separately. There are efforts underway to link social and environmental audits, and to relate these fields to audits to determine product quality.

Terminology

What are integrated audits? Integrated audits are based on an integrated standard, with one standard covering a multiplicity of issues. Combined audits cover two or more standards within an audit. For example, companies are currently asking auditors to combine Social Accountability 8000 (SA8000) audits with ISO9000 (which relate to quality) or ISO14000 audits (which relate to environment).

The benefits of integrated audits

Combined audits save both time and money. Rather than preparing for several audits, a company concentrates its efforts on one audit cycle. According to Fitz Hilaire, Director of Global Supplier Development at Avon, dovetailing audits minimizes disruption in factories. Preparing for audits often results in lost production time, a phenomenon known as a "short," when production runs short as a result of a slow down in the assembly line.[4]

THERE ARE INHERENT SYNERGIES BETWEEN SOCIAL AND ENVIRONMENTAL AUDITING

Combined and integrated audits will eventually lead to dovetailed or integrated management systems, thereby streamlining these processes. It will be much easier to implement additional management systems once there is one working system in place. According to Dominique Gangeux of BVQI, combining audits for quality and social issues makes it easier to get worker co-operation. Auditors can first discuss with workers what they do – then ease into the more difficult area of social conditions.[5]

One of the barriers to combined audits is training. The skill set of the auditor and team managers who would issue a triple certificate is still not developed.[6]

There are inherent synergies between social and environmental auditing. In fact, there is a clear synergy between ISO14000 and SA8000 in the specific area of Health and Safety since auditors look closely at those environmental issues which might impact directly or indirectly the health and well-being of the workers. Such areas would typically involve the use of toxic chemicals such as toluene in the manufacture of footwear and the variety of herbicides, pesticides, and nematicides which are commonly used in agricultural fields. There are also synergies between social, environmental, and quality auditing.

Are triple certificates in the future?

"One difficulty is that triple certificates would need to be approved by all accreditation agencies, which is unlikely at this point – SGS staff doubt that all of the different accreditation firms would approve a common system. All of these audits require a different skills base.[7]

Quality, social, and environmental auditing are very different. Social auditing relies heavily on interviews, whereas they are not as important in other types of audits. Quality audits require only minimal interviews with workers, limited to several questions about their awareness of certain procedures. In SA8000 auditing, worker interviews constitute important objective evidence. While the agenda is different for quality audits, the record check could be integrated. The management review is similar for both. Pauline Cheung of SGS, one of the first auditors to receive training in SA8000, ISO9000, and ISO14000, believes that

"It's easier to integrate SA8000 with ISO systems in implementation than it is to integrate them at the auditor level.[8]

It's easier for an ISO-certified company to know requirements for SA8000 audits. Some areas are similar, such as control of suppliers. A company with ISO9000 would already have a system in place for controlling suppliers and record-keeping, etc.

There is still a great deal of work to be done to integrate the environmental, social, and quality arenas. Most of the work in this area combines environment and quality auditing. A number of organizations are working to integrate social and environmental issues. The Forestry Stewardship Council (FSC) uses a number of social criteria in certifying if wood is sustainably harvested. MPS, a Dutch-based accreditation firm which provides guarantees that flowers are ecologically-friendly, is seeking to integrate elements of SA8000 into its environmental audits.

AccountAbility 1000 (AA1000) provides a framework for companies seeking to integrate social and environmental issues. AA1000 specifies a process, rather than specifying performance criteria, as does SA8000. The AA1000 requires extensive stakeholder dialogue and reporting.

A number of SA8000 members are already combining SA8000 with other standards. Otto Versand already combines SA8000 auditing with ISO9000 and ISO14000 auditing. Dole is planning to integrate SA8000 with both ISO9000 and ISO14000.

Researchers at the Center for Sustainable Development at the University of Ghent are conducting pilot audits which combine social and environmental issues.[9] In partnership with the Dutch Fair Trade Charter, the Center for Sustainable Development uses the following methodology.

First, the auditors request a written inventory of data on codes and policies, as well as documentation about wages and accidents. Interviews are conducted at the following levels:

- management
- workers
- environment co-ordinator
- safety co-ordinator
- chief of personnel
- medical personnel
- trade unions or worker representatives
- interested parties.

Auditors ask questions on the following issues: environment, freedom of association, child labor, wages, working hours, forced labor, and discrimination. Interviews corroborate information.

Integrated and combined audits are a major issue for corporate social responsibility, with major ramifications for reporting and management systems.

The convergence of standards

SA8000 was developed to provide a single, global standard on workers' rights. Over the course of several years, a number of more limited standards have emerged that are either national or regional and/or sectoral. The multiplicity of standards is confusing to suppliers who have to work in a morass of acronyms. Few companies operate in one sector alone or in one market.

As workplaces around the world are audited, companies will seek to alert consumers to the progress being made in the social arena. **There is a danger that the wide range of codes will confuse consumers, which could lead to indifference and skepticism. Convergence is imperative for both consumers and suppliers alike.**

Fitz Hilaire of Avon predicts the following scenario: companies will require suppliers to conform to one of several comparable standards. The various standards-setting organizations will share data and findings and auditing techniques will improve across the board. SAI is committed to co-operating in the development of strategies for mutual recognition and support among social accountability, standard setting and accreditation organizations and monitors.

Improving the SA8000 system

Continuous improvement is an integral aspect of SA8000 and SAI seeks to continuously improve the standard and the verification system based on the results of stakeholder consultation. There are several processes underway for continuous improvement. SAI actively seeks advice and input on SA8000 through consultations, workshops, pilots, and through the Internet. A review committee of the Board then decides which changes will be made. Thus far, the comments received have been very useful and insightful. A revised version of SA8000 is already available.

SAI is also developing a panel of experts to advise on how to apply SA8000 in agriculture. The agricultural sector poses several challenges including the high degree of seasonality, the difficulty of auditing wide tracts of land, the lack of management systems, and the use of vast numbers of small suppliers. SAI has conducted pilots audits on SA8000 in the agricultural setting. With the advice of a panel of experts, SAI is drafting an Agricultural Supplement to the *Guidance Document*.

The challenge of partnership

SA8000 requires concerted action by a wide variety of players: NGOs, trade unions, governments, consumer organizations, and international organizations all have important roles to play in improving workers' rights around the world. Companies cannot make major changes without partnerships. SA8000 is an agent of change, a catalyst to promote human rights and workers' rights, that can foster the necessary partnerships to create change. The alliances developed by stakeholders to implement SA8000 will have important ramifications in promoting development around the world.

This section examines the role of each major player and then provides models of the types of partnerships that need to develop to make workplaces more humane.

The role of governments

As the role of governments shrinks around the world, aid to the South is shrinking. Governments increasingly seek to leverage their aid with private sector efforts. SA8000 seeks to address employment issues with significant consequences for development. As such, SA8000 is of great interest to many governments in both the North and South. Several governments in the industrialized world are developing strategies for promoting awareness of SA8000, while governments in the South are looking to promote SA8000 to make their exports more competitive.

There are several roles that governments can take in promoting SA8000. Aid agencies, both national and multilateral, can assist small and medium-sized companies in meeting SA8000. There is a precedence for this, as governments have provided assistance to companies seeking to implement ISO standards. Governments can use SA8000 in their procurement of goods and services. Governments can also fund training for NGOs, trade unions, and workers. There is also a significant amount of research to be done on wages. Governments in the South can also promote better working conditions by enforcing existing legislation and strengthening National Labor Inspectorates.

The role of consumers

Consumers play a vital role in pressing for better working conditions around the world. SAI is working to inform consumers about the SA8000 verification system and how they can encourage more companies to commit to a social accountability program. To this end, SAI is developing information materials adaptable for use in a public service campaign, and materials for SA8000 member companies to use in stores, on hang-tags, and in catalogs.

The role of NGOs

"NGOs can mobilize other groups such as local communities, local government units, learning institutions, and even labor unions to campaign for the implementation of and compliance with the standard. NGOs can also help small and medium-sized enterprises adopt the standard. The sector has its own resources and technologies that it can utilize to assist these enterprises in implementing SA8000. NGOs themselves can be trained to conduct auditing among companies, especially small and medium-sized ones that cannot afford to employ the bigger audit firms. The sector provides a necessary perspective, and can lend greater credibility, to the audit process. Finally, NGOs can become brokers of information. Like labor unions, they usually have access to information that may be valuable in verifying – or negating – audit findings."[10]

SAI is working to build capacity among NGOs to facilitate their participation within the SA8000 system: in addition to building NGO participation on the SAI Advisory Board, SAI is planning to conduct pilot audits with NGOs in three countries and provide training for local suppliers, with NGO and trade union participation.

The role of trade unions

Trade unions have a critical role to play in promoting SA8000. The SA8000 standard empowers union members in their work. At the SA8000 workshop in Brazil, trade union leaders felt that trade unions had neglected to get involved in ISO system, and had suffered as a result. Trade unions are currently seeking to implement training programs for their members on SA8000. Trade unions also have a significant role to play in developing SA8000 guidance in other sectors.

SAI and the International Textile, Garment and Leather Workers' Federation (ITGLWF) are seeking to train 6000 workers in 12 countries in Asia, Africa, and Latin America about how they can use workplace codes of conduct to their benefit. The goals of this project are as follows.

- To promote greater trade union participation in the analysis, development, and monitoring of voluntary corporate codes of conduct, using the Social Accountability 8000 (SA8000) standard on workplace conditions as a study model.

- To encourage international and regional co-operation among trade unions in order to facilitate transnational co-operation and help workers better articulate their concerns to business and government.

The various sectors mentioned above bring different resources and talents. Partnerships between these sectors are a powerful agent of change. The challenge will be to develop partnerships with co-ordination and convergence so as not to splinter key players into polarized groups nor confuse the public and the business community.

The rise of a hybrid auditor

Currently, there are two types of social auditors: traditional auditors and NGO representatives. Both of these bring essential expertise to the task of auditing, while also facing challenges. Auditing is both a science and an art. Traditional auditors know the science of auditing and have the training to view facts objectively. However, traditional auditors tend to be male, whereas factory workers in assembly plants tend to be predominantly female. Traditional auditors typically come from professional background, possibly hindering their ability to have frank discussions with young workers. NGOs have a close link to the community, but few of them have been trained as auditors. Their ties to the community may make them less than objective.

Through the global organizations they work for, professional auditors are able to deliver audits around the world. NGOs, for the most part, are local and cannot audit around the world. For a company with 10,000 suppliers in 30 countries, it is extremely difficult to contract with dozens of NGOs to audit.

The future of SA8000 involves the establishment of a new type of auditor: the hybrid auditor, who combines the training of the professional auditor, with the sensitivity of the NGO. In many cases, this fusion is beginning to occur. NGOs are participating in auditor training sessions to learn the mechanics of auditing.

The hybrid auditor will have both a local and a global ("glocal") perspective. An interesting example of the new type of auditor is COVERCO, the Commission for the Verification of Codes of Conduct in Guatemala. Upon auditing a supplier for Liz Claiborne International in Guatemala, COVERCO found that neither the workers nor the management of the factory understood the Liz Claiborne code of conduct, known as its Standards of Engagement. In addition to recommending training, COVERCO came up with a local solution: creating a cartoon version of the code known as the "Code Comix." Designed by a local graphic artist in Spanish, the Comix is user-friendly.[11]

In the coming years, it is likely that local auditing firms and NGOs will form partnerships with their counterparts in other countries and regions, leading to the creation of a "glocal" NGO which provides auditing services. According to David Schilling of The Interfaith Center for Corporate Responsibility (ICCR), a global alliance of NGO monitors is developing in Central America.[12]

Any organization can become accredited to audit SA8000. SAI is working with a number of local NGOs to assist them in becoming accredited. According to Eileen Kohl Kaufman, Executive Director of SAI, SAI is seeking mechanisms to subsidize local NGOs, while providing incentives for joint ventures.[13]

New legislation

What is considered to be best practice today, will be considered a mandatory part of doing business in the future.

"The UK is considering a new company law framework, which will require large companies to put at the heart of their annual reports a statement of purpose, and their values, their key relationships, their policies, and their targets for social, ethical, and environmental performance. The logic behind this is that it is now recognized that business success does depend upon success in each of the key relationships."[14]

Companies adopting SA8000 now will be ahead of the competition when new legislation emerges compelling them to be more socially responsible.

Conclusion

Social Accountability 8000 is the most widely accepted standard for creating a humane workplace at the global level. Fully operational for two years, companies are implementing SA8000 in more than 14 countries around the world. The combined annual revenues of these companies exceeds $106 billion. SA8000 is on its way to becoming universally accepted, as it translates across borders and industry sectors.

As the case studies in this book demonstrate, SA8000 provides a practical approach to ensuring that companies and their suppliers are using humane practices. Furthermore, as the case studies of Avon and WE Europe illustrate, this book demonstrates that the business benefits associated with SA8000 outweigh the costs of audits. Increased productivity and product quality, combined with enhanced employee morale are some of the business benefits of adopting SA8000. But the greatest driver is the cost of non-compliance, doing nothing to address the social side of the supply chain exposes companies, placing their reputation at risk.

SA8000 was developed through a stakeholder approach, where groups with vastly different points of view have agreed to a basic set of principles and a methodology for auditing social concerns. Trade unions, NGOs, and companies from many countries have developed SA8000 through consensus.

SA8000 combines the conventions from the International Labour Organization with the methodology of ISO, the International Organization on Standardization. A hybrid of ILO and ISO, SA8000 is unique among other social codes. The marriage of ISO and ILO will facilitate implementation for companies that already have certifications on quality and environment, while driving the integration of social concerns with environmental and quality issues. Moreover, SA8000, like ISO standards, has a set of management systems to ensure thorough implementation of social norms.

New legislation and growing consumer awareness are forcing companies to examine social issues within their companies and throughout their supply chains. Companies are faced with a choice: become a leader in building a more humane workplace or risk being exposed for abusing workers' rights and human rights.

SA8000 is a dynamic code, which will continue to evolve through consultations around the world. There is still a significant amount of work to be done to develop a system for implementing SA8000 in agriculture and other sectors. Most of all, SA8000 is predicated on a process of continuous improvement. Please send any suggestions or feedback on the standard or this book to Deborah Leipziger at thehague@wanadoo.nl.

What can companies do to implement SA8000? First, contact Social Accountability International at 30 Irving Place, New York, NY 10003 or visit the website at www.sa-intl.org for information. As an introductory measure, companies can take a training course on SA8000 and dialogue with companies already adopting SA8000. The staff at SAI are available to assist member companies in implementing SA8000.

Skeptics say, "What can a manager or company do about large social issues such as child labor and discrimination?" SA8000 provides the answers. As Margaret Mead once wrote: "Never doubt that a small group of committed citizens can change the world. Indeed, that is all that can."

Appendix

Resources

For information on training and ordering publications, contact:

Social Accountability International
www.sa-intl.org
30 Irving Place
NY NY 10003
USA
TEL: 1-212-358-7697

Production facilities that seek certification to the SA8000 humane workplace standard must contact one of the organizations accredited by SAI to certify compliance to the SA8000 standard and arrange for an audit. Below are the organizations accredited to certify compliance to SA8000, as of February 2001.

SGS-ICS (International Certification Services)
John Brookes
Meadows Office Complex
210 Route 17 North
Rutherford, NJ
USA
TEL: 1-201-935-1500
FAX: 1-201-935-4555

DNV (Det Norske Veritas)
Sangem Hsu
Room 3204, Tower I
Admiralty Centre
18 Harcourt Road
Hong Kong
TEL: 852-2528-9168
FAX: 852-2529-5805

BVQI (Bureau Veritas Quality International)
Sophie Goodall
224–226 Tower Bridge Court
Tower Bridge Road
London SE1 2TX
UK
TEL: 44-(0)20-7661-0700
FAX: 44-(0)20-7661-0790

ITS (Intertek Testing Services)
Larry Berson
70 Diamond Road
Springfield, New Jersey
USA
TEL: 1-973-346-5500/7081
FAX: 1-973-379-5232

UL (Underwriters Laboratories Inc.)
Steve Cohan
Quality Registration Services
12 Laboratory Drive, PO Box 13995
Research Triangle Park, NC 27709
USA
TEL: 1-919-549-1305
FAX: 1-919-547-6200

To order the Compass self-assessment CD ROM, contact:

Compusense
cba@compuserve.nl
TEL: 31-(0)71-519-0326

For information on other codes of conduct, contact:

Clean Clothes Campaign
www.cleanclothes.org
PO Box 11584
1011 GN Amsterdam
The Netherlands
TEL: 31-20-4122785

Ethical Trading Initiative
www.ethicaltrade.org
78–79 Long Lane
London EC1A 9EX
UK
TEL: 44-(0)20-7796-0515

Fair Labor Association
www.fairlabor.org
1401 K. St. NW
Washington DC, 20005
USA
TEL: 1-202-898-1000

Worldwide Responsible Apparel Production (WRAP)
PO Box 10673
Arlington, VA 22210
USA
TEL: 1-877-524-WRAP (US); 1-703-524-8209

For assistance on communicating about social policies:

Global Reporting Initiative
11 Arlington Street
Boston, MA 02114
USA
TEL: 1-617-266-9389
www.globalreporting.org

AccountAbility/Institute for Social and Ethical Accountability
www.AccountAbility.org.uk
Thrale House
44–46 Southwark Street
London SE1 1UN
UK
TEL: 44-(0)20-7407-7370
Secretariat@AccountAbility.org.uk

Key interested parties

Amnesty International prepares annual surveys by country which deal with human rights issues. Amnesty International, 1 Easton Street, London WC1X 8DJ, UK. 44-(0)20-7413-5500, Fax: 44-(0)20-7956-1157, or 600 Pennsylvania Ave. SE, 5th floor, Washington DC, 20003, 1-202-544-0200, Fax: 1-202-546-7142, www.amnesty.org

Anti-Slavery International has written studies on forced and bonded labor throughout the world. ASI also has studies on child labor in Nepal, Portugal, Italy, the UK, and Morocco. An excellent resource is: *Helping Business to Help Stop Child Labor*: ASI, ISDN: 900918381, www.antislavery.org

Business for Social Responsibility is a membership organization which promotes corporate social responsibility: 609 Mission Street, 2nd floor, San Francisco, CA 94105, USA, 1-415-537-0888, Fax: 1-415-537-0889, www.bsr.org

CEP is a research organization which analyzes the social and environmental record of companies: 30 Irving Place, NY, NY 10003, USA, 1-212-358-7697, Fax: 1-212-358-7723 www.cepaa.org

Child Labor Coalition is a network of 50 labor and consumer groups working to end the exploitation of children in the workplace. They publish *Child Labor Monitor* and are part of the National Consumers League, 1701 K. St. NW, Suite 1200, Washington DC 20006, USA, 1-202-835-3323, Fax 1-202-835-0747, www.nclnet.org / clc.htm

European Initiative for Ethical Production and Consumption is a four-party European forum based on European-level partnership between the main social and economic players who wish to encourage ethical production and consumption. The goal of the IEPCE is to help companies and other organizations to adopt and implement appropriate codes of conduct through information, training, and the exchange of good practice. 8 rue Joseph Stevens B-1000, Brussels, 32-2-502-7767, Fax 32-2-502-8064, www.iepce.org

Human Rights Watch conducts research on prison labor by prisoners of conscience. www.hrw.org

IEPCE – see European Initiative for Ethical Production and Consumption

Interfaith Center on Corporate Responsibility
Room 550
475 Riverside Drive
NY, NY 10115
USA
TEL: 1-212-870-2928

The International Confederation of Free Trade Unions is a network of 124 million workers in 143 countries. They have 213 trade union centers around the world, which can assist companies in attaining information on union rights. The ICFTU can be reached at: Boulevard Emile Jacqmain 155, Brussels, Belgium, B-1210, 32-2-224-0333, www.icftu.org.

International Labour Organization has an excellent resource for companies – ILOLEX – which contains all the ILO Conventions and Recommendations. www.ilo.org, Route des Morillons 4, 1211 Geneva 22, Switzerland. The ILO's International Programme on the Elimination of Child Labour (IPEC) has offices in over 24 countries. For addresses of country offices, contact: ipec@ilo.org Geneva, 41-22-799-6827, Fax 41-22799-8771.

International Organization for Standardization
www.iso.ch.
1 rue de Varembé
Case postale 56
CH-1211, Geneva, 20
Switzerland
TEL: 41-22-749-0111

International Social and Environmental Accreditation and Labelling Alliance
(ISEAL) seeks to develop common protocols for the monitoring of social and
enviornmental codes. Members include: SAI, the Forestry Stewardship Council,
the Marine Stewardship Council, the Fair Trade Labelling Organization, and
other organizations. ISEAL Secretariat, www.isealalliance.org, c/o Falls Brook
Center, 125 S. Knowlesville, New Brunswick, E7L 1B1, Canada.

The US Department of Labor's Bureau of International Labor Affairs has
several volumes on child labor. The most recent is: *By the Sweat & Toil of Children:*
Volume V which details efforts to eliminate child labor in the following
countries: Bangladesh, Brazil, Egypt, Guatemala, India, Kenya, Mexico, Nepal,
Nicaragua, Pakistan, Peru, the Philippines, South Africa, Tanzania, Thailand, and
Turkey. This volume is available at: US Department of Labor, International Child
Labor Program, Room S5303, Washington DC, 20210,
www.dol.gov/dol/ilab/public/programs/iclp.

Social Accountability International Advisory Board Members June 2000

Fundacao Abrinq Pelos Direitos da Crianca
Oded Grajew
Instituto Ethos
Brazil

Amalgamated Bank
Mr Jack Sheinkman
Chairman of the Board
Amalgamated Bank

Amnesty International
Morton Winston, PhD
Professor of Philosophy
The College of New Jersey

Avon
Mr Fitz Hilaire
Director, External Development

CIM/Groupe/Promodes
Bertrand Duliscouet
Quality & Packaging General Manager
France

City of New York
The Honorable Alan G. Hevesi
Alternate: Steve Newman, First Deputy

Social Accountability International
Ms Alice Tepper Marlin
President
Social Accountability International

Dole Food Company
Sharon E.H. Hayes
Director of Environmental Affairs

Eileen Fisher
Mr David Zwiebel
VP for Special Projects

International Textile, Garment and Leather Workers' Federation
Mr Neil Kearney
Secretary General
Belgium

Legacoop Nazionale
Ivano Barberini
Presidente
Italy

Maquila Solidarity Network
Lynda Yanz
Canada

National Child Labor Committee
Ms Dorianne Beyer
General Counsel
National Child Labor Committee

Otto-Versand
Dr Johannes Merck, VP
Germany

SGS-ICS
Mr Jeffrey Horner
SGS Senior Vice President
Switzerland

Toys "R" Us
Mr Tom DeLuca
Director, Product Development and Safety Assurance

Trillium Asset Management
Mr Simon Billenness
Research Analyst
Trillium Asset Management

UNI
Union Network International
Jan Furstenborg
Switzerland

UNOPS
(United Nations Office for Project Services)
Mr Reinhart Helmke
Executive Director

WE Europe BV.
Mr Frits Nagel
The Netherlands

Notes

Chapter 1

1. "SA8000: Another Measurement of Corporate Success," *ActionLINE*, June 2000, p. 25.

2. Brad Brown and Meredith McNabb, Interview with Marie-Pierre Daniel and Patrick Guerin, Celtipharm, May 24, 2000, p. 1.

3. *Ibid.*

4. Heather White, "Monitoring in China," in *Visions of Ethical Sourcing*, Financial Times Prentice Hall, edited by Dr Raj Thamotheram, p. 47.

5. "SA8000: Another Measurement of Corporate Success," *ActionLINE*, June 2000, p. 24.

6. Centre for Tomorrow's Company (1997), *The Inclusive Approach and Business Success* quoted in Mark Goyder and Peter Desmond, "Is ethical sourcing simply a question of good supply-chain management?," *Visions of Ethical Sourcing*, London: Financial Times Prentice Hall, p. 27.

7. M. Goyder and P. Desmond, "Is ethical sourcing simply a question of good supply-chain management?," in Dr Raj Thamotheram (ed.), *Visions of Ethical Sourcing*, London: Financial Times Prentice Hall, p. 28.

8. *Ibid.*

9. *Ibid.*, p. 30.

10. Brown and Meredith, p. 1.

11. Brad Brown, Susan Perry and John Wheeler, *Corporate Social and Environmental Responsibility: Protecting Shareholder Value by Protecting Corporate Reputation*, December 15, 1999, pp. 4–5.

12. Fitz Hilaire, "Visionary Leadership which makes a critical difference," Presentation given at CEPAA Brussels Conference, December 6, 1999.

13. This cost can be quoted by certification bodies listed in the Appendix.

14. Research conducted by Environics International of Canada, quoted in *Visions of Ethical Sourcing*, p. 5.

15. Andrew Ward, "Companies come under pressure to alter course of ethical investment" in *Financial Times*, July 8, 2000.

16. Hilary Sutcliffe, *Soft Issues, Hard Cash: The risks and rewards of corporate responsibility*, Working Draft, September 15, 2000, p. 35. See also A. Ward, "Companies come under pressure to alter course of ethical investment," *Financial Times*, July 8, 2000.

17. *Ibid.*, p. 35.

18. Sutcliffe, *Soft Issues, Hard Cash: The risks and rewards of corporate responsibility*, p. 34.

19. While there are other differences between the ISO and SA8000 systems, it is not necessary to analyze other differences in detail at this time.

20. Except for exceptional and short-term business circumstances.

21. *Seminar Report from CEPAA Consultative Workshop, SA8000: Social Responsibility for Companies*, São Paulo, Brazil, June 16–18, 1999, p. 6.

22. Chapters 2 and 7 provide examples of how companies can communicate to the public about SA8000.

23. *Assessment of the Fair Labor Association Agreement of November 2, 1998.* International Labor Rights Fund, January 1, 1999.

24. The WRAP standard in these areas requires the following:

*"**Environment**: Apparel manufacturers will comply with environmental rules, regulations, and standards applicable to their operations, and will observe environmentally conscious practices in all locations where they operate.*

***Customs compliance**: Apparel manufacturers will comply with applicable customs law and, in particular, will establish and maintain programs to comply with customs laws regarding illegal transhipment of apparel products.*

***Drug interdiction**: Apparel manufacturers will co-operate with local, national, and foreign customs and drug enforcement agencies to guard against illegal shipment of drugs.*

25. Business for Social Responsibility has developed a chart which compares all aspects of the various systems.

Chapter 2

1. Presentation by Fitz Hilaire, "Managing Workplace Practices in the New Era of Social Responsibility, CEPAA Conference, Brussels, December 6, 1999.

2. Presentation by Fitz Hilaire at CEPAA Conference, December 6, 1999.

3. Presentation by Robert Cowling, CEPAA Conference, December 6, 1999.

4. Presentation by Alessandra Vaccari to Advisory Board of SAI, July 7, 1999.

5. The Global Compact was proposed by UN Secretary General Kofi Annan to unite the UN and the private sector to promote environment, labor standards, and human rights. See www.unglobalcompact.org for more information.

6. Correspondence between Sharon Hayes and the author, November 12, 2000.

7. "Good Supplier Relationships," presentation by Amy Hall and Eileen Fisher, at CEPAA Annual Conference, Brussels, December 6, 1999.

8. *Ibid.*

9. Questionnaire completed by Amy Hall and Eileen Fisher, December 22, 1999, p. 4.

10. An HMO is a privately-owned health care provider.

11. Rugmark carpets are certified as having been made without child labor.

12. "SA8000: A Critical Assessment from the Viewpoint of Otto Versand," (Powerpoint presentation) December 1998.

13. Presentation by Achim Lohrie at CEPAA Annual Conference in Brussels, December 6, 1999.

14. *Ibid.*

15. *Ibid.*

16. CEPAA Questionnaire completed by Achim Lohrie, Otto Versand, December 12, 1999, p. 4.

17. CEPAA Advisory Board Notes: July 8 and 9, 1999.

18. Code of Conduct for "WE Europe," Utrecht, December 1998.

17. Presentation by Frits Nagel, WE Europe, at Nyenrode University, conference sponsored by Business Ethics Department, June 2, 1999.

20. CEPAA Questionnaire completed by Frits Nagel, November 15, 1999.

Chapter 3

1. "Child Labour in the World," fact sheet from *Abolishing Extreme Forms of Child Labour*, Geneva: ILO, 1998.

2. *Ibid.*

3. *Guidance Document for Social Accountability 8000*, SAI, November 10, 1999, p. 16.

4. *Ibid.*

5. *Ibid.*

6. Homeworking is the term for factory work done at home, often sewing or assembly.

7. *Guidance Document*, p. 17.

8. Examples of such practices are discussed in Chapter 6.

9. Interfaith Center on Corporate Responsibility, Fact-Finding Report on Footwear Manufacturing, Nike and Reebok Plants in Indonesia, Vietnam, China, March 1–12, 1998. *The Corporate Examiner*, Vol. 26, Nos 9-10, July 31, 1998, p. 7.

10. *Guidance Document*, p. 25.

11. *Fact-Finding Report on Footwear Manufacturing*, ICCR, p. 12.

12. "Sexual Harassment in the Workplace," *World of Work: The Magazine of the ILO.*, on www.ilo.org/public/engligh/235press/magazine/19/sexhar.htm, last updated April 30, 1997.

13. Roger Zegers de Beijl, *Combatting discrimination against migrant workers: International standards, national legislation and voluntary measures – the need for a multi-pronged strategy*, International Labour Organization, Conditions of Work, Paper presented for the Seminar on Immigration, Racism and Racial Discrimination, Centre for Human Rights, Geneva, May 5–9, 1997 p. 1.

14. Interview with Dominique Gangneux, BVQI, November 21, 2000.

15. E-mail correspondence from Dominique Gangneux, BVQI, November 27, 2000.

16. *Guidance Document*, p. 30.

17. Questionnaire completed by J. Kusima, Kesko, November 1999.

18. Neil Kearney: presentation at CEPAA's Conference, December 6, 1999. Brussels.

19. *Guidance Document*, p. 30.

20. The ILO and United Nations Habitat Programme publish statistics on what the average household needs to spend per person. One source is: *Household Income and Expenditure Statistics, 1979–1991.* No. 4, ILO, Geneva, 1991.

21. *Guidance Document*, p. 30.

22. Interview with Dominique Gangneux, BVQI, November 21, 2000.

Chapter 4

1. Interview with Mark Miller, Corporate Business Manager, Global Program for Social Accountability, SGS, November 22, 1999.

2. Section II includes ILO conventions on forced labor (pp. 29 and 105), freedom of association (p. 87), right to collective bargaining (p. 98), equal remuneration for male and female workers for work of equal value, discrimination, as well as workers' representatives, minimum age and recommendation, occupational safety and health, vocational rehabilitation and employment of disabled persons (p. 159), and homework (p. 177), and the Universal Declaration of Human Rights, and the UN Convention on the Rights of the Child.

3. *Guidance Document*, p. 44.

4. Questionnaire for Companies Implementing SA8000, completed by Frits Nagel, WE Europe, completed November 15, 1999, p. 2.

5. *Ibid.*

6. Note: The WE Europe Code of Conduct mirrors SA8000, but also includes several environmental issues, see the case study on WE Europe, p. 36.

7. Interview with Mark Miller, SGS, November 22, 1999.

8. Consultative Workshop: *SA8000 Social Responsibility for Companies*, Report from the seminar held on June 16–18, 1999, in São Paulo, Brazil, p. 4.

9. *Fact-Finding Report on Footwear Manufacturing*, ICCR, p. 12.

10. While homeworking is not disallowed under SA8000, a facility that uses homeworking cannot be certified.

11. This is not required under SA8000, but is a useful indicator of whether there is over-time.

12. This is not required under SA8000, but is a useful indicator of the time periods where over-time is required and how long these intervals are. An awareness of these schedules can help to organize production schedules so as to prevent long periods of time where over-time is necessary.

Chapter 5

1. Definition from a UN document from 1994, cited in P.J. Simmons (1998), "Learning to live with NGOs," *Foreign Policy*, p. 83.

2. If there is evidence of violations, interested parties can appeal against the decision to certify a company or the accreditation of a certification firm.

3. Paddy O'Reilly and Sophie Tickell (1999), "TNCs and Social Issues in the Developing World" in M.K. Addo (ed.) *Human Rights Standards and the Responsibility of Transnational Corporations*, The Hague: Kluwer Law International, p. 280.

4. Sune Skadegard Thorsen (1999), "Strategies for the Application of Human Rights to Business," in M.K. Addo (ed.) *Human Rights Standards and the Responsibility of Transnational Corporations*, The Hague: Kluwer Law International, p. 199.

5. "Learning to Live with NGOs," p. 90.

6. "Pakistan's soccer-ball industry: After the children went to school," *The Economist*, April 8, 2000, p. 81.

7. *Ibid.*

8. *Ibid.*

9. For a deeper look into this case study and other partnerships see

M. McIntosh, D. Leipziger, G. Coleman, and K. Jones, (1998), *Corporate Citizenship: Successful strategies of responsible companies*, London: Financial Times Pitman Publishing, p. 217.

Chapter 6

1. Cherry Fajardo (2000) *Consultative Workshop in Southeast Asia on SA8000, 25–27 August 1999*, Hotel Rembrandt, Quezon City, Philippines, "*Workshop Report*, CEPAA," pp. 3–5.

2. "Shareholder Groups Ally in Anti-Sweatshop Cause" in *IRRC Corporate Social Issues Reporter*, October 2000, p. 4.

3. Human Rights Watch, *A Job or Your Rights: Continued sex discrimination in Mexico's maquiladora sector,* December 1998.

4. Rijk van Haarlem, "Monitoring in the Workplace," presentation given at US Department of Labor and ILO conference: Advancing the Global; Campaign Against Child Labor: Progress Made and Future Actions Conference, May 17, 2000, US Department of Labor, video available on DOL website.

5. Note that while total population estimates are for 1996, child labor data are from several years.

6. Barton Gellman, "AIDS in Africa: The deadliest plague, West refused to heed early warnings of pandemic," Washington Post Service, *International Herald Tribune*, July 6, 2000, p. 2.

7. Heather White, Letter to the Editor, *Human Rights Dialogue*, Carnegie Council on Ethics and International Affairs, Winter 2001, Series 2, Number 5.

8. David Hecht, "In Senegal, a clothier's crumpling: Local woes idle factory transplanted from the US, *International Herald Tribune*, February 10, 2000, p. 9.

9. *Measuring the Social Accountability of Business in Central and Eastern Europe: A Consultative Workshop on SA8000*, March 4–6, 2000, Budapest, Hungary, CEPAA, p. 12.

10. *Ibid.*, p. 11.

11. "The People Trade," *Newsweek*, July 3, 2000, p. 18.

12. Gertrude Stein's famous poem says "a rose is a rose is a rose."

13. Nancy Cleeland, "Garment makers compliance with labor laws slips in Los Angeles," *Los Angeles Times*, quoted in *Campaign for Labor Rights bulletin*, September 27, 2000.

14. Lee Tucker, *Fingers to the Bone: United States failure to protect child farmworkers*, Human Rights Watch, NY: June 20, 2000.

15. Lance Compa, "US workers' rights are being abused," *Washington Post*, October 30, 2000, citing his study for Human Rights Watch: *Unfair Advantage: Workers' Freedom of Association in the US Under International Human Rights Standards.*

16. *Ibid.*

Chapter 7

1. Advisory Board meeting, New York, March 8, 1999.

2. *AccountAbility 1000, A Foundation standard for quality in social and ethical accounting, auditing, and reporting*, September 1999, The Institute of Social and Ethical Accountability, p. 30.

Chapter 8

1. Questionnaire completed by Jouko Kuisma, Kesko, November 1999.

2. Written interview with Marisa Parmigiani with author, SMAER, January 19, 2000.

3. Phone interview with Mark Miller, Corporate Business Manager, Global Program for Social Accountability, SGS, November 22, 1999.

4. Presentation by Fitz Hilaire, "Visionary leadership which makes a critical difference," CEPAA Annual Conference, Brussels, December 6, 1999. (Available on SAI website, www.SA-intl.org)

5. Interview with Dominique Gangneux, Product Manager, BVQI, January 17, 2000.

6. Interview with Mark Miller, formerly Corporate Business Manager, Global Program for Social Accountability, SGS, November 22, 1999.

7. *Ibid*.

8. Interview with Pauline Cheung, Marketing Manager of SGS Hong Kong Ltd, December 7, 1999.

9. E. Borgo, B. Mazijn and S. Spillmaeckers, "*An Integrated Approach to Chain Analysis for the Purpose of Chain Management by Companies,*" Center for Sustainable Development, University of Ghent, July 2000.

10. SA8000 Workshop in the Philippines, *CEPAA Report*, 1999, p. 11.

11. Homero Fuentes and Dennis Smith, "Independent monitoring in Guatemala: what can civil society contribute?," in Dr Raj Thamotheram (ed.), *Visions of Ethical Sourcing*, London: Financial Times Prentice Hall, p. 42.

12. "Shareholder Groups Ally in Anti-Sweatshop Cause," *Corporate Social Issues Reporter*, IRRC, October 2000, p. 3.

13. *Ibid*., p. 4.

14. M. Goyder and P. Desmond, "Is ethical sourcing simply a question of good supply-chain management?," in Dr Raj Thamotheram (ed.), *Visions of Ethical Sourcing*, London: Financial Times Prentice Hall, p.35.

Index